Biotechnology and Competitive Advantage

Biotechnology and Competitive Advantage

Europe's Firms and the US Challenge

Edited by
Jacqueline Senker

Science Policy Research Unit, University of Sussex, UK

Coordinated by
Ronald van Vliet

Ministry of Economic Affairs, The Hague, The Netherlands

Edward Elgar
Cheltenham, UK • Northampton, MA, USA

Published by
Edward Elgar Publishing Limited
8 Lansdown Place
Cheltenham
Glos GL50 2HU
UK

Edward Elgar Publishing, Inc.
6 Market Street
Northampton
Massachusetts 01060
USA

A catalogue record for this book
is available from the British Library

Library of Congress Cataloguing-in-Publication Data
Biotechnology and competitive advantage: Europe's firms and the US
    challenge / edited by Jacqueline Senker; co-ordinated by Ronald van
    Vliet.
        Includes bibliographical references.
        1. Biotechnology industries—European Union countries.
    2. Biotechnology industries—United States. 3. Competition,
    International. I. Senker, Jacqueline.
    HD9999.B443E8513 1998
    338.4'76606'094—dc21

                                                                    97-38251
                                                                        CIP

ISBN 1 85898 739 3

Printed and bound in Great Britain by Bookcraft (Bath) Ltd

Contents

Figures

Tables

Contributors

Rohini Acharya is a Trade Policy Analyst at the World Trade Organization, Geneva. Her main research interests are in international trade, trade policy and technological change, with a specific emphasis on biotechnology and biodiversity. She has published widely on these topics and is writing a book on biotechnology and biodiversity, to be published by Edward Elgar.

Anthony Arundel is a Research Fellow at MERIT, University of Limburg. His major research area is the innovative behaviour and strategies of manufacturing firms. He has used both large-scale surveys and smaller, more focused studies to evaluate a wide range of issues related to innovation, including the role of the public research infrastructure, patents and appropriability, and external sources of knowledge.

Gerald Assouline is the Director of QAP Decision, a small consultancy company in Grenoble. He also lectures on Technology Management at the University of Grenoble and on Sustainable Development at ISARA (Engineering Agronomic School) in Lyon. His main research interests are science and technology policy assessment, strategic issues in biotechnology analysis, health and environmental risk evaluation and management of new agricultural techniques and has published widely on these topics.

Joanna Chataway is a Lecturer in the Development Studies Group at the Open University. Her research interests include technology strategy, technology policy, and the relationship between technology and economic and social policy. She has carried out several research projects related to biotechnology. She also works in the area of development management. She has worked in Western and Eastern Europe, Southern Africa and Latin America. She is co-editor of *Investigative Methods for Policy Related Research: Finding out Fast* (Sage, forthcoming 1998).

Jacqueline Estades is Professor of Sociology at ENESAD (Dijon) and Research Associate at INRA/SERD (Grenoble). Her research focuses on studying the coordination of actors in partnerships between public research laboratories and industry and, more generally, on the organization of R&D.

Pierre-Benoît Joly is Director of Research at INRA/SERD, University of Grenoble. He holds a degree in agricultural engineering (1982) and received a PhD in economics from the University of Toulouse (1987). His main areas of interest are industrial economics, the socio-economics of innovation, and biotechnology. He has published extensively on these issues and is also involved in advisory activities for various national and international institutions. He lectures at the University of Grenoble and ENGREF, Paris.

Marie-Angéle de Looze was Head of Information Services of the Department of Economics and Sociology at INRA (Grenoble) from 1983 until 1992. Since 1993 she has been a researcher at SERD, and specializes in scientometrics, technology watch and competitiveness intelligence.

Paul Martin holds a degree in zoology and was involved in molecular biology research at the MRC Mammalian Development Unit between 1982 and 1989. He subsequently worked on health and social policy issues before joining the Science Policy Research Unit, University of Sussex in 1992. He will shortly complete his PhD on the social shaping of gene therapy technology. Research interests include the sociology of technology, innovation in medical technology and the social control of biotechnology.

Luigi Orsenigo is Associate Professor of Economics at Bocconi University, Milan. His research interests are in industrial economics and the economics of technical change. He is author of *The Emergence of Biotechnology* (Pinter Publishers, 1989) and of several articles in books and in leading international journals in his field.

Shyama Ramani is a Research Associate at the Institut National de la Recherche Agronomique in France. She holds a doctorate degree in economics from Cornell University, USA. Her research centres on the study of R&D cooperation, the evolution of the biotechnology sector and game theory as applied to industrial organization. She also teaches at the Institut National Polytechnique de Grenoble and Université Pierre Mendès-France at Grenoble.

Michael Reinhard is a senior researcher in the Department of Growth and Innovation at the ifo Institute for Economic Research, Munich. He has worked in the area of innovation research, with a focus on the field of biotechnology, for 15 years.

Pier Paolo Saviotti is Director of the INRA/SERD research group, Université Pierre Mendès-France, Grenoble. He previously worked at the University of Manchester, in the Departments of Science and Technology Policy and of Economics. He has been involved in research on the economics of technological change and innovation and on evolutionary theories. He is the author of several articles and books, including *Technological Evolution, Variety and the Economy* (Edward Elgar, 1996) and co-edited *Technological Collaboration* (Edward Elgar, 1996).

Jacqueline Senker is Senior Fellow at the Science Policy Research Unit, University of Sussex, Brighton. Her research interests include studying the interactions between university and industrial research and inter-firm collaborations, with a special emphasis on biotechnology. She has published widely on these topics and is co-author of *Knowledge Frontiers* (Oxford University Press, 1995). She is grateful to the Economic and Social Research Council who contributed towards the costs of preparing this book through their Science, Technology, Energy and Environment Research Programme (STEEP) at the Science Policy Research Unit.

Sandy Thomas is Senior Fellow at the Science Policy Research Unit, University of Sussex, Brighton. Her research interests include biotechnology policy, concentrating on intellectual property rights, new technologies in the pharmaceutical industry and company strategies in biotechnology.

Ronald van Vliet is a political scientist, working as a policy adviser at the Directorate General for Industry of the Ministry of Economic Affairs in Den Haag, the Netherlands. From 1994 to 1997 he worked for the Biotechnology Unit of DG XII (Science, Research and Development) of the European Commission in Brussels. In this function he dealt *inter alia* with issues of the socio-economic impact of biotechnology and was responsible within the Commission for the studies presented in this book.

Abbreviations

ANVAR	Agence Nationale pour la Valorisation de la Recherche (France)
BAP	Biotechnology Action Programme (EU)
BBSRC	Biotechnology and Biological Sciences Research Council (UK)
BEP	Biomolecular Engineering Programme (EU)
BMBF	Federal Ministry for Education, Science, Research and Technology (Germany)
BMFT	Federal Ministry for Research and Technology (Germany), predecessor of BMBF
BML	Federal Ministry for Food, Agriculture and Forestry (Germany)
BRIDGE	Biotechnology Research for Innovation, Development and Growth in Europe (European)
Bt	Bacillus thuringiensis
CATI	Cooperative Agreements and Technology Indicators
CNER	Comité National d'Evaluation de la Recherche (France)
CNRS	Centre National de la Recherche Scientifique (France)
DBF	Dedicated biotechnology firm
DNA	Deoxyribonucleic acid
DTI	Department of Trade and Industry (UK)
EASDAQ	European Association of Securities Dealers Automated Quotation
EC	European Commission
EMEA	European Medicines Evaluation Agency
EPA	Environmental Protection Agency (US)
EPC	European Patent Convention
EPO	European Patent Office
EU	European Union
EZ	Ministry of Economic Affairs (The Netherlands)
FDA	Food and Drug Administration (US)
GMO	Genetically modified organism
ICT	Information and communications technology
IICA	Inter-institutional collaborative agreement
INSERM	Institut National de la Recherche Medicale (France)
IPC	International Patent Classification
LDF	Large diversified firm
MAbs	Monoclonal antibodies

MCA   Medicines Control Agency (UK)
MNC   Multinational company
MRC   Medical Research Council (UK)
NASDAQ   National Association of Securities Dealers Automated
           Quotation National Market System (US)
NGO   Non-governmental organization
NIH   National Institutes of Health (US)
QSEs   Qualified scientists and engineers
PSR   Public sector research
rDNA   Recombinant DNA
RRS   Roundup Ready Soybean
RTD   Research and technological development
SAGB   Senior Advisory Group on Biotechnology (European)
SCI   Science Citation Index
SMEs   Small and medium-sized enterprises
USDA   US Department of Agriculture

1. Introduction

Ronald van Vliet

Current European Commission (EC) biotechnology policy has a strong preoccupation with industrial competitiveness, and this is both old and new. It's old, because throughout the history of the different EC biotechnology programmes, one of the policy objectives has always been to strengthen the European science base to provide the necessary scientific backbone for industrial development. New, however, is the direct and proactive manner in which the EC, supported in this by the member states, addresses industry and tries to enhance its competitive position in the world market. There are several reasons for this change. Some of these are linked to developments in the field of biotechnology and its application by industry; others to an evolution in research and technological development (RTD) policy strategies.

Recent developments in biotechnology knowledge and in the structure of the industry which exploits this are the main focus of the contributions of this volume. These developments can be summarized as the following:

1. A number of breakthroughs at the scientific level, which have the potential to contribute to the solution of societal problems. Hybridoma techniques and recombinant DNA technology, which allow the production of valuable proteins in plants, animals and cells, are examples.
2. The genesis of a range of enterprises involved in biotechnology. These enterprises are rather heterogeneous, not only in size but also in the roles they play in advancing biotechnology, in the types of biotechnology applications they target and, as a consequence of all these factors, in their industrial behaviour. However, these enterprises possess several common features. In general, they are relatively young and small. They produce or process science, so they mainly employ scientists. Furthermore, they generally 'co-produce' and thus operate as part of a network, for example with universities or large enterprises. Finally, they share high expectations of growth and development.
3. The global lead in biotechnology, if not in terms of scientific performance, then certainly in terms of industrial *élan*, is clearly being taken

1

by the United States of America (US). This raises several questions
for Europe. Is there an 'American model' from which Europe can draw
lessons? What are the comparative strengths of Europe, for example
niche markets where Europe can take the lead? What positive contribution can European industry draw from the US lead in the field?
4. Because of its undeniable impact on essential features of everyday life
    (practically in terms of health, safety, supply and quality of natural
    resources, and in principle in terms of its implications for creation and
    re-creation), biotechnology and its applications are subject to inten-
    sive debate in society and heavy scrutiny by public authorities
    compared with other new technologies. Biotechnology's progress as an
    economic activity cannot therefore be only a 'technical fix', but will
    also depend heavily on the balance society manages to strike between
    the interests of producers and scientists, the concerns of citizens and
    interest groups, and regulatory requirements.

The evolution of biotechnology and biotechnology-based sectors is
accompanied by an evolution in policy-making strategy regarding biotechnology. Although these developments are discussed in greater detail in
Chapter 2 by Senker, a focus here on some critical developments in the suc-
cessive EC programmes may clarify how policy making at the European
level responded to the demands of the dynamic biotechnology industry.

As mentioned above, there has always been an implicit focus on industry in the EC's biotechnology programmes. For example, the selection of
the yeast genome sequencing projects as flagships of the programmes was
based on the fact that yeast was a model for many other industrially relevant genomes. It was considered less important that the research funded
was primarily academic, than that the results would become available to
all interested parties, and in particular to industry.

This research approach for the benefit of European industry found
general approval,[1] but it was thought that the needs of the newly emerging biotechnology-based industry justified a more explicit approach. The
outline of this approach is set out in the Communication from the EC to
the European Council and Parliament entitled, *Biotechnology and the
White Paper on Growth, Competitiveness and Employment: Preparing the
Next Stage* (Commission of the European Communities 1994). This not
only acknowledges the utmost importance of a balanced regulatory environment for industrial competitiveness, but it also appeals for RTD
programmes that directly aim at enhanced direct involvement of industry,
and small and medium-sized enterprises (SMEs) in particular. Under the
current biotechnology programme (1994–98), the proposals made in this
Communication have been brought into practice. For example, the cell

factories concept implies that projects must combine inputs from science underpinning the use of cells in industrial processes with those very industrial applications, in order to qualify for funding. The result, as shown by funding statistics under this sector in 1995 and 1996, is that virtually all projects include industrial partners.

Second, the concept of demonstration projects has been introduced. These projects aim to evaluate biotechnological processes in 'real operational circumstances'. They ideally bring together not only technology producers and (potential) users of technologies, but also indirectly involved parties such as regulatory authorities, consumer and environmental organizations, and any other party that may affect the market success of an innovation based on biotechnology (so called 'extended audiences').

Third, a set of measures has been brought in to stimulate SME participation in the RTD programme.

In addition to these measures, which were planned to have a direct impact on industrial participation, activities have been set up that aim both at a better understanding of the societal context of biotechnology and its applications, and at a greater dialogue with consumers, interest groups, education systems, and so on. As mentioned previously, an informed and unprejudiced public attitude towards biotechnology is crucial for its economic success.

Policy makers both in the member states and at the European Union level are well aware that the dynamics of biotechnology-based industry differ drastically from those in other innovative sectors, and that the further development of biotechnology demands appropriate public policies. For that reason, a number of studies selected for funding in 1994 were targeted at improving the understanding of biotechnology-based industrial development, with a view to improving policy design. A number of researchers involved in these studies met in a workshop in Grenoble to discuss and fine-tune their preliminary findings, and some of these findings are presented in this book. Each of the studies looks at the issue of enhancing competitiveness from a different angle.

Chataway and Assouline's study on 'Risk perception, regulation and the management of agro-biotechnologies' (Chapter 4) addresses the issue of the relationship of the industry *stricto sensu* with the societal context in which it operates. Since biotechnology and biotechnology-based products are the subject of intense public debate, the biotechnology industry's economic success requires more than the usual industry management capabilities. Different strategies of risk management for industry use are examined, as well as interactions with societal groups and policy makers responsible for regulatory affairs. The study focuses on the agricultural biotechnology sector, where recently public debate on the implications of biotechnology use has been most intensive, and where the broad regulatory framework is currently under discussion. The principles and mechanisms, however, apply to all fields and applications of biotechnology.

The study presented by Saviotti et al. (Chapter 5) examines factors that influence the start-up and early development of biotechnology enterprises. Apart from a limited number of multinational companies, the 'biotechnology industry' consists almost solely of small and relatively young firms. Saviotti analyses how these firms contribute to the creation of knowledge in biotechnology and, on the other hand, what factors influence their creation.

The contribution by Acharya et al. (Chapter 6) broadens the focus slightly and looks at the networks in which the biotechnology companies operate. Types of collaboration between both public and private entities are analysed, and a comparison is made with the situation in the US. The chapter presents some preliminary observations on the relative importance of different protagonists in the development of competitiveness in biotechnology.

Chapter 7 by Senker et al. focuses on large, multinational firms, mostly in the pharmaceutical sector. A number of these traditionally Europe-based enterprises have increasingly integrated biotechnology knowledge in their processes and therefore tend to look towards the US where biotechnology is more developed. This sector of industry therefore displays most clearly the competitive tension between Europe and the US. As clarified in Senker's study, this tension creates a dynamic and peculiar set of interactions between European and non-European parties, and this affects their respective competitive positions in a more complicated way than is often stated.

Chapter 8 by Martin and Thomas demonstrates many of the points raised in the previous chapters in an analysis of developments in gene therapy commercialization in the UK and the US. Gene therapy is considered to be a technique of enormous potential both for society and the economy. However, its development and applications depend on a complex interaction between scientists, firms specializing in gene therapy, large pharmaceutical firms and policy makers. It is typically an area where the issues to be solved contain the crucial questions that characterize modern biotechnology:

- How can a fragile SME-dominated industry – in this case gene therapy firms – attract the necessary capital and survive financially while awaiting the return on their investment?
- How should the scientific challenge to make the techniques effective, safe and operational for human application be tackled?
- How should public concerns and doubts be dealt with, and how should these be balanced with the needs of scientists and industry in a regulatory framework ?

The chapters based on the studies are preceded by two introductory chapters: one by Senker describing the policy context of biotechnology in Europe, and one by Saviotti providing a more theoretical background to industrial structure, knowledge creation and its dynamics. Acharya summarizes the main findings of the studies in the conclusions to the volume.

By bringing their research results together in this book, the researchers responsible for the studies intend to combine the insights they have developed. They do not pretend to provide an ultimate analysis of current European competitiveness in biotechnology, nor do they pretend to have found a solution to the complicated policy problems in this area. It should be remembered that the individual studies selected for funding by the EC's biotechnology programme, after an independent peer review, were modest in size, scope and methodology. Analyses are usually based on representative but limited samples, and only a limited number of countries could be taken into account in the comparative analyses. Although each of the authors is well known for work of the highest scientific standards, it must be remembered that the studies brought together in this volume sometimes required compromises. As a consequence, the authors wish to stress the limitations of the work in this volume as well as any conclusions that may be drawn.

From the point of view of the EC's biotechnology programme the publication of this book is a valuable contribution to its policy of not only funding high quality projects and studies, but also of disseminating the results to a wider audience. However, it should be stressed that although the EC supported the publication of this book, the statements made by the various authors remain their own responsibility and do not necessarily reflect the policies or policy intentions of any European institution.

NOTE

1. See, for example, Christou et al. (1996).

REFERENCES

Christou, P., N. Carey, H. Brunner et al. (1996), *Evaluation of the BRIDGE Programme (1990–1994)*, EUR 16650 EN, Luxembourg: Office for Official Publications of the European Communities.
Commission of the European Communities (1994), *Biotechnology and the White Paper on Growth, Competitiveness and Employment: Preparing the Next Stage*, COM (94) 219 final, Brussels: CEC.

2. Biotechnology: the external environment

Jacqueline Senker

INTRODUCTION

Europe has fallen behind the US in the commercial exploitation of biotechnology. Developments have differed from member state to member state, and have been affected by numerous factors in the external environment. This chapter seeks to provide a review of the conditions for biotechnology commercialization in Europe, especially those elements which appear to explain varying development between countries, such as the existing structure of industry, the science base, government policy and the regulatory environment.[1]

Biotechnology was first commercialized in the US in the mid 1970s. Concern that a similar phenomenon was not occurring in Europe led to policies aimed at emulating the US example. The first part of this chapter, therefore, deals with the American experience and Europe's response. However, the promise of biotechnology has been rather slow to materialize. The second part of the chapter will consider the factors which are thought to inhibit progress: uncertainty about regulation and patenting, and the European Union's (EU's) attempts to try and develop policies acceptable to member states with very differing approaches to these issues.

The development of biotechnology has been led by academic research, with two scientific breakthroughs in the early 1970s leading to its commercialization. The first was the discovery in 1973 by Herbert Boyer and Stanley Cohen, researchers at the University of California and Stanford University, that deoxyribonucleic acid (DNA) could be cut, recombined and inserted into a foreign bacterium which would then express a new gene. Two years later, Milstein and Kohler of the British Laboratory of Molecular Biology, Cambridge, UK reported the discovery of monoclonal antibodies. Their work involved fusing cells with specific properties and is a method for producing large quantities of specific antibodies.

Robert Swanson, a US venture capitalist, was the pioneer who recognized the commercial potential of biotechnology. His negotiations with Boyer, co-inventor of the gene splicing process, led to the launch of Genentech in 1976 – the first venture capital biotechnology company. The example of Genentech led to the birth of the biotechnology industry in the US, with an explosion of small firms led by academic entrepreneurs who retained close links with their academic base. Early start-up funds were provided by venture capitalists. Venture capital is an American phenomenon which supplies risk capital to new companies based on scientific research. In 1979 there were 250 US venture capital firms, but very few in Europe, except for a handful in the UK (Rothwell and Zegveld, 1982, pp. 37, 89).

Small biotechnology firms created and maintained the US lead in biotechnology. Commercialization was very largely the outcome of a marriage between venture capital and university scientists in a culture which encouraged a close relationship between university science and industry and supported entrepreneurship. The rapid growth of US dedicated biotechnology firms (DBFs) explains the concern that a similar phenomenon was not occurring in Europe, since it was thought that small firms had a key role to play in the commercialization of biotechnology. A variety of other factors were thought to explain Europe's hesitation to exploit biotechnology: lack of venture capital, an underdeveloped science base, lack of knowledge of the new technology and its commercial potential by existing firms and, compared with the US, a rather negative attitude to industry by European academics. The policies adopted by many European countries from about 1980 aimed to rectify the latter three deficiencies by building up the science base in biotechnology, creating links between that science base and industry, and promoting the formation of small firms. Policies were often also directed towards the assimilation of new biotechnology knowledge by large companies in sectors such as chemicals, pharmaceuticals and agro-food. The next section reviews these policies for countries involved in the case studies in other chapters of this book. There were few initiatives to remedy the lack of European venture capital. However, this means of financing spread throughout Europe in the 1980s, and is most developed in the UK, the Netherlands and France (Manigart, 1994, p. 530).

NATIONAL POLICIES FOR BIOTECHNOLOGY

The following brief reviews of national policies for biotechnology focus mainly on attempts to build up the European science base. They also consider the activities of environmentalists in some Northern European countries such as Germany and Denmark, where concern about the safety and ethical implications of genetic manipulation is thought to have held back the industrial exploitation of biotechnology.

Denmark

Denmark is generally regarded as being advanced in biotechnology, mainly because of the activities of two large firms in the pharmaceuticals and brewing industries. Until 1987, however, when an Action Programme for Biotechnology was put in place, it had a weak scientific infrastructure in biotechnology. The Action Plan, which allocated $70 million over five years to build up the biotechnology science base in universities and research institutes, has been succeeded by comparable programmes (Sveinsdottir, 1995). The government also sponsors 14 biotechnology 'centres without walls' to promote interaction between industry and academic research. Industry has been constrained to some extent by environmentalists' opposition to the production of recombinant DNA (rDNA) products and the effect of regulations passed by the Danish parliament in 1986. These regulations have subsequently been somewhat relaxed, but are still considered to be the most stringent regulatory system in existence (US Congress, 1991, pp. 232-3).

France

The majority of basic research in France is organized and funded by Centre National de la Recherche Scientifique (CNRS), a state-funded institution which funds biotechnology research in its own laboratories, in universities and in other research institutes. Three other public research institutes are involved in biotechnology: the Institut National de la Recherche Medicale (INSERM) focuses on health and medical research, the Institut National de la Recherche Agronomique on agricultural research, and the Commisariat á l'Energie Atomique has expertise in biophysics, structural and molecular biology, and bio-informatics. In addition the Institut Pasteur, a private institution, receives considerable income from CNRS and INSERM. Realization that France's position was rather weak in biotechnology led, in 1982, to a Mobilisation Plan. The programme ran for 11 years, with government funding of FF 1.8 billion and a similar amount of industrial investment. Its aim was to strengthen the R&D infrastructure and to encourage French companies to acquire genetic engineering technologies and know-how. The French firms targeted included major conglomerates in pharmaceuticals, agrochemicals and food. A major achievement of the programme is considered to be the construction of new links between industry and universities. Prior to the programme, there was no tradition of technology transfer or collaborative links between industrial and public sector research (US Congress, 1991, p. 234). In 1994 the Comité National d'Evaluation de la Recherche published a report on the Programme Biotechnologie, however, which suggested that there could have been more efficiency in achieving these results. It criticized the programme for a lack of strategic vision and coordination, and for failing to control and evaluate the projects which had been funded (Hodgson, 1994). Biotechnology has now been reintegrated into the general biology funding framework of the Ministry of Research and Technology.

France has a small but growing number of small biotechnology firms (Ramani, 1995, p. 759). Growth appears to have been supported by changes in venture capital availability and government agencies such as the Agence Nationale pour la Valorisation de la Recherche (ANVAR). Venture capital was almost non-existent in France until the late 1980s but has subsequently become easier to obtain. Since 1983 ANVAR, originally established to transfer technology created in the public sector, has provided funds to support the commercialization of public sector research. Such funds include seed capital for start-up firms (Walsh, Niosi and Mustar, 1995).

Germany

There are a multiplicity of sources of funding for biotechnology research in Germany. Biotechnology research is promoted and funded by several ministries, including the Federal Ministries for Education, Science, Research and Technology (BMBF),[2] of Food, Agriculture and Forestry, and of Health, and by the *Länder* (states). Basic research is carried out at universities, Max Planck Institutes, National Research Centres, 'Blue List' institutions,[3] and federal and state research laboratories (Irvine, Martin and Isard, 1990, pp. 53-5).

In the early 1980s biotechnology was not widely used in Germany and there was a lack of well-qualified young scientists. Accordingly, in 1985 the Federal Ministry for Research and Technology (BMFT) set up a programme to help Germany catch up in biotechnology and to increase the numbers of scientists in this area. This 'Applied Biology and Biotechnology' programme (1986–89) financed the Society for Biotechnology Research (a national research centre which receives 90 per cent of its funds from the BMBF) and provided support to four 'Gene Centres' set up by the universities at Munich, Cologne, Heidelberg and Berlin. The programme subsidized small and medium-sized firms' involvement in biotechnology by providing

grants for firms to purchase know-how and services from research laboratories. It also funded the cost of academic research in collaborative research
projects between small firms and academics. The programme was judged to
be a success and, from 1990, was continued and extended with the
'Biotechnology 2000' programme. With German reunification and government policy to develop the biotechnology sector in the new *Länder*, four
additional 'Blue List' institutes are being established in Jena, Magdeburg,
Gatersleben and Halle, specializing in molecular biotechnology, neurobiol-
ogy, plant genetics and plant biochemistry (BMFT, 1989, 1993).

The majority of industrial R&D in biotechnology is conducted by
Germany's large chemical/pharmaceutical multinational companies. Over
the years, however, these companies have faced strong Green Party opposition to plans to open facilities to manufacture recombinant products.
The recommendations of a government commission on genetic engineering, published in 1987, led to a national debate on a proposed 'gene law'
to define the environment within which industry could conduct R&D.
The commercialization environment deteriorated when one *Länd* blocked
an application to manufacture genetically engineered insulin. This decision and other considerations, such as catching up with leading-edge
know-how, influenced several German companies to build manufacturing
and research facilities in the US. Growing realization that lack of a reli-
able legal basis for genetic engineering R&D and manufacturing was
leading to loss of German investment and jobs led to the 1990 Gene
Technology Law. The law was very stringent and placed most of the
responsibility for implementation on the *Länder*, which had no experience in these matters. In late 1993 the law was modified, removing many
implementation barriers (Edgington, 1995, p. 753).

Germany has approximately 75 small biopharmaceutical companies
(Ernst & Young, 1994), but there are still significant barriers to the formation of DBFs in Germany. In addition to Green Party opposition,
which bars pension funds from investing in biotechnology, deterrents
include poor public acceptance of biotechnology, the lack of an entrepreneurial culture among academic scientists and the dearth of German
venture capital firms able to evaluate plans for biotechnology start-ups
(Edgington, 1995, p. 754; Ward, 1995a, p. 1048).

Italy

Government policies for biotechnology started later in Italy than in other
European countries and industrial activity is low. Large chemical companies had capabilities in some older areas of biotechnology, but were
slow to react to the opportunities offered by genetic engineering. Only a

few medium-sized pharmaceutical companies showed interest in the new technology. The Italian science base in biotechnology was also weak. Some centres performed research in areas related to biotechnology, but few were involved in frontier research. These conditions have been explained by the absence of any targeted government intervention for biotechnology before 1987.

In 1986, the Federchimica Report emphasized the need for a comprehensive policy for biotechnology and the National Committee for Biotechnology issued its proposals for a national plan for biotechnology. The government responded by setting up the national plan, 'Advanced Biotechnology' for applied research in 1987, with a budget of 200 billion lire. Half was allocated to biomedical projects and the remainder to bioprocesses for chemical, energy and environmental applications, and for agricultural projects. In September 1995, as the 'Advanced Biotechnology' programme neared its end, a follow-on programme with a budget of 100 billion lire was proposed. Support for basic research and university–industry collaboration was provided by a five year targeted project 'Biotechnology and Bioinstrumentation', launched at the end of 1987, with a budget of 84 billion lire. The programme was intended to be industry oriented, but almost all the research projects were carried out at universities and research institutes, with little industrial involvement. In 1987 the government also intervened in the establishment of a new firm dedicated to biotechnology research, Tecnogen, whose research is funded mainly through public funds from national research programmes (Acharya, Arundel and Orsenigo, 1996, pp. 43–4).

The Netherlands

Dutch research in third-generation biotechnology dates back to the early 1970s, but concern about the risks of rDNA research and a slow response by government to recommendations for the legal regulation of research with clear guidelines led to a ban on rDNA research between 1976 and 1978 (Sharp, 1985a, p. 194). After 1978 the publication of guidelines created a workable environment for rDNA research in the Netherlands. A few years later, government gave active support to biotechnology research in response to the Schilperoort Report (1982) on biotechnology. The report argued that biotechnology would be of great significance to Dutch industry because much of its output was concentrated in sectors which could benefit from biotechnology techniques. For instance, the Netherlands is home to food and agro-chemicals multinationals. Funding was concentrated on the universities and institutes most active in the biological sciences, with support for companies involved in collaborative research with public sector researchers (Senker and Sharp, 1988, pp. 71–3). Dutch policy encourages scientists from the public research sector to establish 'spin-off' firms, but only a handful of these firms have been identified (Gebbart, 1993; Ernst & Young, 1994; EZ, 1994). Recent changes in the organization of funding for Dutch public sector research demands that universities and applied research institutes such as TNO fund a much larger proportion of their activities from European Commission (EC) funds or contracts from the private sector. As a result, the public sector has concentrated its resources into research areas which are closer to the market (Acharya, Arundel and Orsenigo, 1996, p. 61).

United Kingdom

British policy for biotechnology was stimulated by the Spinks Report (Advisory Council for Applied Research and Development/Advisory Board for the Research Councils/The Royal Society, 1980) which highlighted the importance of the technology. There was a fragmented response from the various agencies responsible for university, agricultural and food, and medical research. The most targeted efforts developed in the academic sector, with the 1982 establishment of the Biotechnology Directorate within the Science and Engineering Research Council. The Biotechnology Directorate, which was responsible for funding postgraduate students and academic research in biotechnology, was successful in its aims to foster a programme of strategic university research in biotechnology and to forge links between that research and industry. At about the same time the Department of Trade and Industry (DTI) set up the Biotechnology Unit to raise industrial awareness of opportunities in biotechnology and to encourage more R&D in industry. The Biotechnology Directorate and the Biotechnology Unit developed close links, including shared funding of several programmes of collaborative university/industry research, in which large pharmaceutical, agro-chemical and food multinationals became involved (Senker and Sharp, 1988). A major reorganization of British research funding agencies took place in 1994, which was expressly designed to make public sector research more industrially relevant and to build stronger links with industry. A significant feature of this reorganization was the creation of a Biotechnology and Biological Sciences Research Council (BBSRC), which integrated responsibilities for funding academic, agricultural and food research in these disciplines (Cabinet Office, 1993, p. 29). The results of a Technology Foresight Programme now inform the direction, balance and content of the BBSRC's funding allocations. In 1995, the DTI launched the 'Biotechnology Means Business' initiative – a comprehensive set of measures to help companies, whatever their size or industrial sector, to explore and exploit biotechnology.

Britain has the largest population of small biotechnology firms in Europe. Two DBFs were founded in the early 1980s, on the initiative of the government, to commercialize the results of publicly funded research. The government also intervened in the capital market to increase the availability of venture capital (Walsh, Niosi and Mustar, 1995, p. 316). Growth of the British small firms sector accelerated in the 1990s. Relaxation of the rules for listing by the British Stock Exchange now permits developing biotechnology companies to raise investment funds.

European Union

EU policies for R&D, patenting and regulation affect company decisions about their biotechnology activities. The earliest EU support for biotechnology research dates back to 1981, when the EC introduced the Biomolecular Engineering Programme (BEP), a small four year programme which promoted post-doctoral training and exchange, and projects which linked academic research with industry. Biotechnology was declared a priority area for innovation in 1983 and a working party was set up to develop a joint EC R&D programme (Sharp, 1985b, p. 198). Over time, the EC's investment in biotechnology research increased and BEP was succeeded by various programmes. In some, such as FLAIR or SCIENCE, biotechnology was a subsidiary interest under broader themes. Programmes whose main thrust was biotechnology were the Biotechnology Action Programme (BAP) (1986–89), Biotechnology Research for Innovation, Development and Growth in Europe (BRIDGE) (1990–93) and BIOTECH (1992–98). The focus of most of these programmes has been basic research and, at first, most participants were academic researchers (Malmborg et al., 1988, p. 3). Growing industrial participation reflects EC efforts to increase involvement from this sector.

The EU has also been involved in developing policy for biotechnology patents and for the regulation of biotechnology. Policy making in both these areas is complicated by the fact that biotechnology is a new science and its application raises issues where there is a great deal of uncertainty. In addition, the EU has had to seek harmonization between the various member states' approaches to these issues.

Patents in Western Europe can be obtained either under the separate national laws of individual countries or under the law of the European Patent Convention (EPC). European patents fall under the jurisdiction of the designate states and are enforced in national courts. In 1988 the EC proposed a directive to secure harmony between national regulations and the EPC and to upgrade national patent laws in Europe to US and Japanese standards. The biotechnology industry reacted favourably to the directive because it indicated that the EC was interested in promoting the industry, but member states had many objections to the articles of the proposed directive. An amended proposal was published in late 1992 which was agreed by the Council of Ministers in early 1994. However, the European Parliament voted down the final draft of the Council Directive on the Legal Protection of Biotechnological Inventions in spring 1995. The chief problem with the proposed legislation was its treatment of transgenic plants and species and the ethical issue of whether the patenting of living things should be allowed. The failure of the European Parliament to approve the directive is likely to have only a slight effect on industry, since case law will continue to provide the basis for biotechnology patent protection (Crespi, 1993; Scott-Ram and Sheard, 1995).

In 1990 the European Council of Environment Ministers passed two directives on the regulation of biotechnology – on the contained use of genetically modified organisms (GMOs) (90/219) and on their deliberate release (90/220). These directives, responsibility for whose implementation lies with member states, allow national authorities to interpret and implement them in ways which conform with existing national practice. However, there are major differences in the ways in which member states develop and implement regulations for biotechnology; there are high levels of public participation in decision making in countries such as Denmark and Germany, while there is very little public participation in France and secrecy surrounds the decision-making process (Shackley, 1993). These differing practices have led to tensions between national authorities. The Danes, for instance, were unable to impose more stringent controls than those agreed in the directives; France thought the controls too stringent (Shackley and Hodgson, 1991). The directives have been much criticized. By way of illustration, a UK House of Lords Report on the regulation of GMOs (based on the EC directives) considers that, 'regulation of the new biotechnology of genetic modification is excessively precautionary, obsolescent, and unscientific'. The report calls for relaxation in the terms of both directives and believes that product-based regulation should largely replace the existing process-based laws. It states that, 'GMO-derived products should be regulated according to the same criteria as any other product' and thinks that process-based regulation should only be retained in work involving pathogenic organisms and deliberate release of GMOs outside the low-to-negligible risk category (House of Lords, 1993). The French accept taking a cautious approach to the regulation of GMOs. However, they want a flexible regulatory system, able to respond to growing knowledge which may indicate that more simplified procedures are appropriate.[4] In June 1994 the EC put forward proposals to encourage the development of the European biotechnology industry. The proposals include amending the directives so as to take account of the recognition that risks to human and environmental safety are lower than was thought when the directives were adopted (Jones, 1994). However, as with the patent directive, mixed views across the Community make it difficult to reach a clear-cut decision.

A unified European regulatory system for approving medicinal products has been developing over time. In the period to 1992, the UK and France were the preferred regulatory authorities for handling applications with an EU-wide interest. Preference was based on their ability to process applications expeditiously and on having a high level of international credibility with regulatory authorities in other major markets. Since 1995 the EC approval process has come under the aegis of the European Medicines Evaluation Agency (EMEA). Procedures differ for non-biotechnology and biotechnology medicines. There are decentralized procedures for non-biotechnology medicine, under which approval in one member state is recognized by all the others. Any disputes are resolved by EMEA. Centralized procedures are mandatory for biotechnology products, and optional for other 'high tech' products. Applications from manufacturers for approval are made directly to EMEA. Product approvals by EMEA are valid in all member states (Griffin, 1995).

The Food and Drug Administration (FDA) is responsible for approving new drugs for the US market, including those which have been approved for use outside the US. Potential new drugs must, from the outset, be produced in facilities approved by the FDA. US companies perceive major differences between the role which EMEA and the FDA have adopted towards regulatory approval for biopharmaceuticals. The FDA is perceived to be concerned with both a drug's safety and its efficacy. By comparison, EMEA is thought to concentrate on product safety and allow the market to decide whether the product is efficacious. In consequence clinical trials and their evaluation are considered to be quicker and cheaper in Europe than in the US (Ward, 1995b). There are currently moves afoot in the US for legislation to reform the FDA, with hopes of bringing US requirements into line with Europe (Holzman, 1995), and the EU, US and Japan are now working together through the International Conference on Harmonization to recommend practical ways to achieve greater harmonization of quality, safety and testing requirements (EMEA, 1996, p. 8).

CONCLUSIONS

This review of the external environment for commercializing biotechnology in Europe describes some of the obstacles faced and the steps taken by the EU and its member states to overcome them so as to catch up with the US. The remainder of this book will reflect the industrial response to these conditions in 1995. It is worth recording continuing efforts in Europe to remove various obstacles to the industrial exploitation of biotechnology. During 1996 the European Parliament has been considering a revised directive on patenting from the EC which takes ethical concerns into account, and this directive could be approved by the end of 1997 (Anon., 1996, p. 15). Proposed changes to the EU's directive on the contained use of GMOs will bring it very close to US guidelines, and discussions between the EC and industry are underway about amendments to the directive on the deliberate release of GMOs into the environment (Ward, 1996, p. 133). 1996 also saw the opening of the European Association of Securities Dealers Automated Quotation (EASDAQ), modelled on the US National Association of Securities Dealers Automated Quotation National Market System (NASDAQ).

NOTES

1. The conditions described are those pertaining in 1995. Subsequently, significant changes have and are occurring, particularly at a European level. These are mentioned in the conclusions to this chapter.
2. The former Federal Ministry for Research and Technology (BMFT).
3. A loose confederation of research institutes, the functions of which vary between providing services (museums, libraries), carrying out basic or medical research and, in some cases, applied research.
4. Personal communication from French expert, 1996.

REFERENCES

Acharya, R., A. Arundel and L. Orsenigo (1996), *The Evolving Structure of the European Biotechnology Industry and its Future Competitiveness*. Final Report for the Biotechnology Programme (BIOTECH) of the European Community, DG XII, the Netherlands: MERIT.

Advisory Council for Applied Research and Development/Advisory Board for the Research Councils/The Royal Society (1980), *Biotechnology. Report of a Joint Working Party*, London: HMSO.

Anon. (1996), 'Another chance for bio-patenting', *Research Fortnight*, 16 October, 14–15.

BMFT (Der Bundesminister für Forschung und Technologie) (1989), *Programmreport Biotechnologie*, Bonn: BMFT.

BMFT (Der Bundesminister für Forschung und Technologie) (1993), *Bundesbericht Forschung*, Bonn: BMFT.

Cabinet Office (1993), *Realising Our Potential: A Strategy for Science, Engineering and Technology*, CM2250, London: HMSO.

CNER (Comité National d'Evaluation de la Recherche) (1994), *Un Autre Regard sur la Recherche, Sept Evaluations 1990–1993*, partie 7 Evaluation du programme 'Biotechnologie', Paris: La Documentation Française.

Crespi, R.S. (1993), 'Protecting biotechnological inventions', *Chemistry & Industry*, No. 10, 363–6.

Edgington, S. (1995), 'Germany: a dominant force by the year 2000?', *Bio/Technology*, **13**(8), 752–6.

EMEA (1996), *Directory*, Luxembourg: Office for Official Publications of the European Communities.

Ernst & Young (1994), *European Biotech 94. A New Industry Emerges*, London: Ernst & Young International.

EZ (Ministerie van Economische Zaken) (1994), *Biotechnologiebeleid: Van Onderzoek naar Markt*, Den Haag: Project Groep Biotechnologie, MEZ.

Gebbart, F. (1993), 'The Netherlands pursues the goal of becoming Europe's biotechnology delta', *Genetic Engineering News*, 15 May, 12–13.

Griffin, J.P. (1995), 'The EMEA – Euromouse or white elephant?', *Scrip Magazine*, March, 9–10.

Hodgson, J. (1994), 'The end of French biotechnology R&D?', *Bio/Technology Europroduct Focus*, Spring, 5.

Holzman, D. (1995), 'Political consensus to bring reform by spring', *Chemistry & Industry*, No. 20, 823.

House of Lords Select Committee on Science and Technology (1993), *Regulation of the United Kingdom Biotechnology Industry and Global Competitiveness*, HL Papers 80-I and 80-II, London: HMSO.

Irvine, J., B. Martin and P. Isard (1990), *Investing in the Future. An International Comparison of Government Funding of Academic and Related Research*, Aldershot: Edward Elgar.

Jones, N.R.N. (1994), 'Relaxing European regulations,' *Bio/Technology*, **12**(11), 1144.

Malmborg, C., P. Feillet, F. Kafatos, J. Koeman, P. Saviotti, G. Schmidt-Kastner and G. Walker (1988), *Evaluation of the Biomolecular Programme – BEP (1982–1986) and the Biotechnology Action Programme – BAP (1985–1989)*, Luxembourg: Commission of the European Communities.

Manigart, S. (1994), 'The founding rate of venture capital firms in three European countries (1970–1990)', *Journal of Business Venturing*, **9**(6), 525–41.

Ramani, S. (1995), 'The French evolution of biotechnology', *Bio/Technology*, **13** (8), 757–9.

Rothwell, R. and W. Zegveld (1982), *Innovation and the Small and Medium Sized Firm*, London: Pinter Publishers.

Schilperoort, R.A. (1982), *Innovative Programme Biotechnologie*, Voor-lichtingsdienst, The Hague: Wietenschapsbelerd.

Scott-Ram, N. and A.G. Sheard (1995), 'The rise and fall of the EU patent directive', *Bio/Technology*, **13**(8), 734-5.

Senker, J. and M. Sharp (1988), *The Biotechnology Directorate of the SERC. Report and Evaluation of its Achievements – 1981–87*, Report to the Management Committee of the Biotechnology Directorate, Brighton: Science Policy Research Unit, University of Sussex.

Shackley, S. (1993), *Regulating the New Biotechnologies in Europe*, DPhil Thesis, Brighton: University of Sussex.

Shackley, S. and J. Hodgson (1991), 'Biotechnology regulation in Europe', *Bio/Technology*, **9**(11), 1056–61.

Sharp, M. (1985a), *The New Biotechnology: European Governments in Search of a Strategy*, Brighton: Sussex European Papers, University of Sussex.

Sharp, M. (1985b), 'Biotechnology: watching and waiting', in M. Sharp (ed.), *Europe and the New Technologies*, London: Pinter Publishers, pp. 161–212.

Sveinsdottir, S. (1995), 'Bridge to biodevelopment', *Bio/Technology*, **13**(8) 763–4.

US Congress, Office of Technology Assessment (1991), *Biotechnology in a Global Economy*, Washington, DC: US Government Printing Office.

Walsh, V., J. Niosi and P. Mustar (1995), 'Small firm formation in biotechnology: a comparison of France, Britain and Canada', *Technovation*, **15**(5), 303–27.

Ward, M. (1995a), 'In Germany, biotech resistance leads to progress', *Bio/Technology*, **13**(10), 1048–9.

Ward, M. (1995b), 'Should the FDA emulate Europe's EMEA?', *Bio/Technology*, **13**(7), 636–8.

Ward, M. (1996), 'Another push to revise Eurobiotech directives', *Bio/Technology*, **14**(2), 133–4.

3. Industrial structure and the dynamics of knowledge generation in biotechnology

Pier Paolo Saviotti

Biotechnology is not an industrial sector, but a set of techniques for the manipulation of living organisms which comprises several disciplines which provide the scientific foundations for such techniques. Both the techniques and the scientific disciplines are used for a wide variety of applications, ranging from pharmaceuticals and agriculture to the environment. It is thus appropriate to talk about biotechnology-based sectors.

Aside from its applications, which have enormous potential scope, a very important feature of biotechnology-based sectors has been the development of a new form of industrial organization, mainly based on highly knowledge/science-intensive small and medium-sized enterprises (SMEs) and a sharply increasing frequency of inter-institutional collaborative agreements (IICAs). While these developments are by no means unique to it, biotechnology has been one of the areas of knowledge which has given rise to the largest number of IICAs (see, for example, Hagedoorn and Schakenraad, 1990, 1992). This poses a series of questions which are important both from a theoretical point of view and in terms of the policy implications for the development of biotechnology.

First, are such forms of industrial organization temporary or permanent? We have to remember that until the beginning of the 1980s economic theories predicted that the only stable forms of industrial organization were markets and hierarchical organizations. Alliances and IICAs were then considered to have only an unstable and temporary existence. The recent upsurge of IICAs constitutes a challenge for economic theory, a challenge to which it has for the moment made only a partial response.

Second, the distribution of SMEs specialized in biotechnology is very asymmetric, having initially been limited exclusively to the US, and even now being skewed towards that country.

Third, given the considerable heterogeneity of the final applications of biotechnology we cannot automatically assume that the same form of industrial organization would be stable and efficient in all biotechnology-based sectors.

These three points suggest that there are a number of potential determinants of industrial organization. To begin with, some of the developments mentioned above are common to all countries where biotechnology has achieved a substantial diffusion. All these countries show a high science intensity, a frequent pattern of collaboration between public research institutions and private firms, and the presence of SMEs/dedicated biotechnology firms (DBFs). The factors which determine these common developments must be present everywhere, although possibly to different extents. The asymmetries that are found in the development of biotechnology can then be explained either by the uneven distribution of these same factors or by some other factors which exist only in some countries.

The very high degree of science intensity of biotechnology-based sectors and applications seems to imply an important role for the dynamics of knowledge generation and accumulation in determining the predominant forms of industrial organization. Also, the uneven distribution of the factors linked to such generation and accumulation seems to be a potential explanatory variable for the relative strengths and weaknesses of biotechnology in different countries. In spite of the importance of knowledge, other complementary factors are involved, for example venture capital. This chapter discusses the main determinants of industrial organization in biotechnology.

THE ENTRY OF NEW FIRMS

An extremely important role seems to have been played by new firms in the commercial development of biotechnology (see, for example, the studies by Kenney, 1986 and Grabowsky and Vernon, 1994 for the US; and Orsenigo, 1989 and Oakey, 1990 for the UK). The empirical evidence of the important role played by SMEs/DBFs in the development of biotechnology implies that there must be particular conditions of entry in the biotechnology-based industries.

Traditionally firm entry is expected to be determined by the presence of more than normal profits. However, even in the presence of supra-normal profits, firms face a number of barriers to entry. Profitability constitutes at best a motivation that is a necessary but not a sufficient condition for entry. In particular, profitability could not explain the entry of firms into completely new industries and technologies. Schumpeter ([1912] 1934) pointed out that entrepreneurs setting up new firms based on radical innovations are motivated by the expectation of the temporary monopoly they will enjoy during the initial period of diffusion of the innovation, when imitation is still limited. In this sense the industrial dynamics of a completely new technological field such as biotechnology, are expected to be different to those of industrial sectors based on more mature technologies. Winter (1984) distinguished between an entrepreneurial and a routinized technological regime, and argued that they give rise to different entry and innovation opportunities for new and incumbent firms. In an entrepreneurial technological regime the underlying knowledge conditions tend to be particularly asymmetric, leading to strongly diverging evaluations about expected profits. By contrast, under the routinized technological regime, less knowledge asymmetry tends to result in innovative activity occurring within the boundaries of the incumbent enterprises (Audretsch, 1995, p. 40). Moreover, to the extent that non-transferable experience is an important input in generating innovative activity, incumbent firms will tend to have an advantage over new firms (Gort and Klepper, 1982).

A number of potential barriers to entry into the biotechnology-based industries exist. For example, although the speed of access to new forms of knowledge may favour SMEs/DBFs with respect to incumbent large, diversified firms (LDFs), often the new forms of knowledge cannot be used alone. Biotechnology may provide novel routes to existing and to new pharmaceutical products, but the technical knowledge required must be combined with knowledge of the approval procedures, of marketing and so on. Such additional forms of knowledge, or complementary assets (Teece, 1986), are possessed by the LDFs which in the past dominated the biotechnology-based industries. The need for complementary assets thus continues to represent a barrier to entry.

Another important barrier to the commercial development of biotechnology is constituted by the risks inherent in the use of genetic engineering and in particular in the introduction of genetically modified organisms into the environment. The regulations adopted to control such risks can have an important effect on the development of biotechnology. Such regulations are by their very nature barriers to the introduction and diffusion of biotechnology. What is particularly relevant is that regulations do not affect all the important actors in the same way. Thus countries having stricter regulations may experience a slower economic development of biotechnology-based industries. Moreover, once established, regulations become an important component of the economic environment of firms. Knowledge of regulations can be more easily acquired by LDFs than by SMEs. Regulations can then become further barriers to entry.

Firm performance in the biotechnology-based industries is thus determined by a number of factors, some of which favour entrants, such as
their faster access to new knowledge, and others which favour incumbents, such as complementary assets and their differential ability to adapt
to regulations. As a result of this situation the entry of SMEs/DBFs has
been very important in the creation of modern biotechnology, but it has
not completely replaced the role played by incumbent LDFs.

Altogether we can say that the biotechnology-based industries have
gone through a period of considerable turbulence during which many
new entrants have made a considerable impact on industrial structure.
Entry of DBFs did not replace incumbents, though some incumbents
either left or became far less prominent. This turbulence led to the formation of a new core of innovators composed of some of the incumbents
and the few entrant DBFs that managed to survive and to grow. However,
a large number of SMEs/DBFs survive with more specialized roles, thus
contributing to innovation in the biotechnology-based industries without
being part of the core of innovators.

As already pointed out, any analysis of the biotechnology-based industries needs to take into account IICAs. Thus the actors previously mentioned
are not independent, but rely to a very considerable extent on IICAs. This
may explain the survival of large numbers of SMEs/DBFs which fail to grow
and to become vertically integrated producers. There are other roles that
SMEs/DBFs can play, such as being intermediaries in knowledge transfer
between public research institutions and LDFs, or exploring the frontiers of
knowledge, a point to which we shall return later in this chapter.

We end this section by observing that among the factors determining
entry and industrial structure in the biotechnology-based industries some
are relatively traditional, such as the presence of complementary assets and
the importance of regulations, while others have recently changed more
radically. In the latter category there is the emergence of new forms of
knowledge linked to the progress of molecular biology which are radically
different from those previously used in the biotechnology-based industries
(for example, organic chemistry). We therefore now discuss the role of
knowledge as a determinant of entry in the biotechnology-based industries.

BIOTECHNOLOGY AND KNOWLEDGE

Absorption Capacity and the Local Character of Knowledge

Firms use a set of competences and elements of knowledge which collectively can be called their knowledge base, which is different from the sum

of the knowledge elements owned by their members. Such a knowledge base must be continuously changed to the extent that scientific and technological changes external to the firm take place. Such external developments, produced by research organizations, can have a wide or narrow range of applications. For example, information technology or biotechnology have a very wide range of applications and are called generic technologies. The knowledge thus created constitutes the external knowledge base of a particular technology, for example biotechnology. This external knowledge base is in principle available to all potential entrants into the biotechnology-based industries. However, as has become clear in recent research, entry is by no means easy or costless. In order to internalize some knowledge firms need to have particular competences and a given knowledge base. Thus past R&D determines the absorption capacity of firms (Cohen and Levinthal, 1989, 1990). In other words, there is a complementarity between the internal knowledge of firms and the external knowledge they want to acquire. This is a consequence of the local character of knowledge which can be expressed by saying that the probability that a firm can incorporate some external knowledge is inversely proportional to the difference or distance between internal and external knowledge. In other words, the greater the similarity between the knowledge already possessed by the firm and the external one, the higher the probability of acquiring the latter (Saviotti, 1996).

Technological Discontinuities and Entry Conditions

The previous considerations have a number of interesting implications. First, firms will continue to use their existing knowledge base as long as they can. This is not just a question of attitudes, but it depends on the value of the investment already in place in the pre-existing technology (see, for example, Henderson, 1993; but such effects were already considered in vintage models of diffusion). However, if a radically new technology with important potential applications is discovered, firms having a high degree of commitment to a pre-existing one will be unable to acquire the new technology. Moreover, if the new technology can partly or completely substitute for the old one, the competences and knowledge base corresponding to the old technology suddenly lose their economic value. This has been described by Tushman and Anderson (1986) as competence-destroying technological change.

A discontinuity of this type has been caused by the emergence of molecular biology and the set of techniques called genetic engineering. There has been some discussion about how new biotechnology is (see, for example, McKelvey, 1994). It is clear that while some biotechnologies (for example, beer or yoghurt making) are very old, the greatest potential for growth and development is linked to the applications of molecular biology and genetic engineering. The problem then is to see how these applications relate to other components of the knowledge base required to use biotechnology. If we take the example of the pharmaceutical industry, where the largest percentage of the investment has gone so far, we can see that the first applications (human insulin, human growth hormone) were substitutes for pharmaceutical products which were previously produced by different processes. In a more general sense, even if we consider completely new pharmaceutical products, a large part of the knowledge and competences involved in bringing the new products to market (for example, legal, marketing, and so on), are common to products obtained by means of older technologies (for example, organic chemistry). In other words, biotechnology is only one of the components of the knowledge base required in the pharmaceutical industry, but it could be considered as its core competence (Prahalad and Hamel, 1990). It can be considered a core competence because (1) it is difficult to acquire, and (2) there are no other ways of obtaining certain results. The other components of the knowledge base required by a firm to take a pharmaceutical product from research to market are called 'complementary assets' (Teece, 1986). If the same complementary assets in the old production processes (for example, organic chemistry-based pharmaceuticals) are required in the new biotechnology-based processes, then LDFs have a considerable chance of survival. The new knowledge replaces only a component, however important, of the overall knowledge base of the LDFs. Moreover, Chesnais and Walsh (1994) point out that in the chemical-related complex of industries, on which biotechnology is having an important impact, the simultaneous existence of more than one technological paradigm has been the rule rather than the exception. Thus the synthetic route to pharmaceuticals has not completely replaced the extractive route, which consisted of obtaining pharmaceuticals from natural organisms. New biotechnologies have revolutionized R&D, but have had a more limited impact on the other activities leading to the production and commercialization of products.

In terms of the previous analysis the situation in biotechnology can be described as follows. Pre-existing firms (usually LDFs) had a knowledge base located in older technologies. Entry into biotechnology was comparatively easier for SMEs/DBFs, especially if among their founders there were biotechnologists. However, SMEs/DBFs cannot easily acquire the complementary assets (for example, marketing, legal) required to integrate vertically. There is, at least for a period, a potential complementarity between the roles of the SMEs/DBFs, which are faster learners in biotechnology, and those of LDFs, which have the complementary assets required to bring products to the market. Such complementarity may not last forever, depending on the rate at which LDFs are able to internalize biotechnology. For the time being it seems that, while LDFs are slowly learning (Grabowsky and Vernon, 1994), there is still considerable scope for SMEs/DBFs in the US. We can expect that LDFs located in imitating countries will experience the same obstacles previously encountered by their US counterparts in learning biotechnology, possibly aggravated by any lags which exist in those countries in developing molecular biology and genetic engineering knowledge. At the beginning of the development of genetic engineering, the main differences between imitating countries and the US were the considerable delays in developing basic knowledge and in the creation of SMEs/DBFs. European LDFs had substantial links into local public sector research which enabled them to recruit and build up in-house expertise (Senker, 1996). However, in the 1970s and 1980s European public sector research lagged behind the US. This led European LDFs interested in acquiring specific biotechnology skills and techniques to invest in US research institutes or DBFs (see Chapter 7 and Senker, Joly and Reinhard, 1996). While at the time this occured European LDFs had no other choice, this pattern of investment may have contributed to slowing down further the creation and development of European SMEs/DBFs in biotechnology. A vicious circle in which the scarcity of scientific potential inhibits the creation of SMEs/DBFs, which in turn fails to stimulate the creation of venture capital units and locks the system into a backward state, would have been the likely outcome if the system had been allowed to evolve spontaneously. In these conditions the only possible form of compensation is public programmes which sponsor the creation of the basic building blocks of the system (for example, Walsh, Niosi and Mustar (1995) for European countries and Canada). A certain extent of catching up with the US has taken place, although the gap does not seem to have been closed. As will be seen in subsequent chapters, forms of collaboration between European LDFs and SMEs/DBFs exist, but these are not necessarily as well developed as possible and they have not replaced alliances with US firms. Hence while we can foresee a role for European SMEs/DBFs as knowledge intermediaries, this role may have been reduced by the early investment of European LDFs in the US. Again, such a pattern of investment, while probably necessary at the time, may have caused a number of structural difficulties in the development of European biotechnology (see Chapter 7 regarding these problems).

Apart from the inter-country differences discussed above, we can reflect on the future stability of an industrial structure comprising not only LDFs but also SMEs/DBFs as a fundamental component. The duration or permanence of such patterns in time is linked to the rate of development of basic biotechnological knowledge. A very fast rate of development could create a semi-permanent obstacle to learning for LDFs and justify the continuation of the present complementarity. As already mentioned, the scientific and technological frontiers in biotechnology are still moving ahead, and this is likely to preserve a role for SMEs/DBFs in biotechnology for the foreseeable future.

Here it must be pointed out that radical technological changes, leading to paradigmatic transitions, can suddenly make the knowledge bases of existing organizations obsolete and create better entry conditions for new firms. Established and large firms may face differential barriers to entry, represented by their rigidity and the inability to adapt to new technological developments. Incumbent firms may have an advantage over new firms in mature technologies to the extent that their previous R&D enhances their absorption capacity of new knowledge (Cohen and Levinthal, 1989, 1990). Such complementarity between internal and external knowledge breaks down when a new technological paradigm appears. The previous knowledge base of the incumbent firm may become redundant or even constitute a barrier to the absorption of the new technology. However, if, as pointed out above, the new knowledge is only a component of the overall knowledge base required to operate in an industry, the rapid entry of new firms may not be accompanied by the disappearance of older ones, but by a complementarity between the two. In summary, we can say that the dynamics of knowledge generation and use can be an important influence on the emerging industrial structure in biotechnology. In particular, and especially in the early stages of the development of the biotechnology-based industries, particularly favourable conditions can be expected to exist for the entry of new firms.

Knowledge Base, Learning and Firm Development

Technological discontinuities can create favourable conditions for entry, but the subsequent development of the firm may depend on other factors. As will be discussed in greater detail in the next section, in order to develop firms have to change the nature of their competences and their knowledge base. For example, if they want to become vertically integrated producers they have to acquire a range of skills in, for instance, marketing, financial and legal matters, and to diversify their products. They can acquire these new competences in two ways: first, they can hire people, and second, they can collaborate with other firms and with public research laboratories. These two modes of learning can be considered internal and external, respectively. However, this distinction is excessive because very often people with advanced specialized knowledge are not hired through the market, but through networks. In other words, the patterns of interaction, or the networks in which SMEs/DBFs participate, are essential for their development (see, for example, Liebeskind et al., 1995). There is thus a dynamic relationship between the knowledge base of a firm and its participation in networks. Given the previously mentioned complementarity between internal and external knowledge, the knowledge base constitutes a necessary condition for learning. On the other hand, the knowledge base is augmented by learning, which implies participation in networks. A given level of knowledge base is required to participate and to gain an advantage from participation in networks. In turn, the knowledge base of the firm is generally augmented by such participation. Furthermore, as already mentioned, the knowledge base is formed by patterns of interaction and communication between the employees of the firm, in addition to individual competences. Of course, the development of the firm is not purely a matter of competences. SMEs/DBFs which seek to grow require financial capital and must develop a strategy and a structure which were not necessarily there at the beginning, particularly if the firm was founded by a scientific entrepreneur. Several studies have identified lack of capital availability as one of the factors constraining the development of SMEs/DBFs in Europe (see, for example, Walsh, Niosi and Mustar, 1995). The US, in comparison, has many venture capital companies as well as access to capital through the National Association of Securities Dealers Automated Quotation. Furthermore, access to sources of financial capital is dependent on pre-existing participation in financial networks.

Regarding the development of strategy and structure, the SME/DBF may have to undergo radical internal changes in management style and composition in order to grow. If the firm begins in a very narrow market niche, growth prospects may be limited, unless differentiation takes place. On the other hand, differentiation is likely to be successful only if it is sufficiently focused and coherent. Moreover, firms that initially carry out R&D only, generally have to achieve at least some extent, however limited, of vertical integration and try to incorporate, for example, production or marketing functions. The major problems confronting many DBFs involved in R&D only, which wish to diversify, is that it takes so long to bring biotechnology products to market.

The Structure of Biotechnology Knowledge

As seen previously, biotechnology can have a very large number of applications in different industrial sectors to the extent of being considered a generic technology. Of course, not all such applications have reached a similar maturity. For example, applications in the pharmaceutical industry seem to be more advanced than in other sectors (for example, plant biotechnology). The question then arises of whether the knowledge base of biotechnology-based firms is relatively homogeneous or whether it is already specialized/differentiated. A paper by McCain (1995) addresses the problem by means of co-classification analysis. She examined the patents and applications of a large number of firms and research organizations within a number of disciplines and subject areas, including microbiology, chemistry, pharmaceuticals, agriculture, cell culture and waste disposal. Using techniques such as multidimensional scaling and cluster analysis she identified five major groupings of companies, research institutions and patent-holding organizations: (1) genetics/other pharmaceuticals/animal cell culture; (2) genetics/fermentation/other pharmaceuticals; (3) fermentation/antibiotics/other pharmaceuticals; (4) biocatalysis/applications; and (5) genetics/cultivation *in vitro*. Such groupings can be arranged in a bidimensional space (see Figure 3.1). The two largest groupings are immediately left and right of the centre, respectively. To begin with, the first cluster of organizations, left of the centre, concerned predominantly with genetics, fermentation and other pharmaceuticals, contains mostly generalist firms taking out more patents than

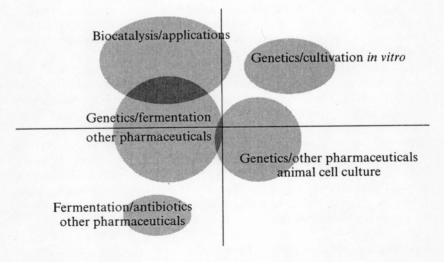

Source: McCain (1995).

Figure 3.1 Approximate reproduction of the five groups of technologies

they publish papers, and producing products such as pharmaceuticals, antibiotics, pesticides, bulk industrial enzymes and other chemicals. The cluster right of centre contains organizations focusing almost exclusively on genetic engineering using animal cell culture and *in vitro* cultivation techniques to develop a wide range of primarily biomedical and agricultural products. If we move from the bottom to the top clusters, we find a progression from medical to non-medical applications. Thus the horizontal axis indicates a movement from fermentation to genetic engineering and the vertical one a movement from medical to non-medical applications. Moreover, using network analysis, McCain found two main foci in biotechnology R&D: fermentation and genetic engineering. This reflects the existence in biotechnology-based industries of several components of the knowledge base, some radically new and some older ones undergoing only incremental innovation.

McCain's study, which seems to confirm some previous findings (for example, Rip and Courtial, 1984), shows that while genetics is a very important component of the knowledge base of virtually all firms and research organizations included in the sample, a differentiation is emerging in which fermentation and genetic engineering on the one hand, and biomedical versus non-biomedical research on the other hand, are the two main organizing dimensions. Chapter 5 includes a comparison of the structure of the biotechnology knowledge base in France and the US, using McCain's approach.

ROLES OF SMEs/DBFs IN BIOTECHNOLOGY

The previous two sections suggest that a particularly important role can be expected in biotechnology for both new and small firms and for technological alliances. Further discussion is required, however, on the question of entry by new firms. A number of distinct roles can be played by SMEs/DBFs, and each role may imply different industrial dynamics. Many SMEs/DBFs aim at becoming vertically integrated producers of, for example, pharmaceuticals, although very few have yet managed to incorporate the required complementary assets. In order to discuss the different roles that can be played by an SME/DBF, we start by describing the development path which leads to a vertically integrated firm. Of course, a newly created firm can hardly be vertically integrated. Typically, biotechnology SMEs/DBFs are founded by scientists (see, for example, Bullock and Dibner, 1995) and at their outset firms are likely to be mainly suppliers of R&D to LDFs. At this stage they would be funded by research contracts or by risk capital. During the second stage,

SMEs/DBFs would concentrate on the development of technologies, while product development would be the objective of the third stage. In this process qualitative changes have to take place in the composition of management and the labour force. Firms are unlikely to grow without integrating at least some complementary assets (for example, marketing), particularly if they attempt to diversify away from their initial output (which may be a specific type of research). They will therefore have to formulate an explicit strategy in terms of output types, partners, markets, and so on. Usually in this process they will require recapitalization, which will involve differentiating their sources of finance and financial capabilities. In this context strategic alliances with LDFs can be very important in providing legitimation and continued growth for SMEs/DBFs.

Very few firms reach the complete vertical integration implied by the three-stage model. In principle, a number of different roles are possible for SMEs/DBFs. At the beginning, firms may exploit a market niche, especially if their product/output type is radically new, or they may find a new route for a pre-existing or slightly modified product. Depending on the nature of the niche, they may behave like Schumpeterian innovators, if the niche has considerable potential and attracts many imitators, or be confined to a niche that is safe from competition, because it is small and without great potential for development. Furthermore, the SME/DBF can simply continue to be a supplier of knowledge services. Various possible roles are summarized below:

- First, an SME/DBF can behave like a *Schumpeterian innovator*, introducing a radical innovation into the economic system, motivated by the expectation of the temporary monopoly that it can enjoy before imitation becomes widespread. During this process what was initially a niche becomes a normal or routine market, from which monopolistic profits disappear. In this case incumbents are often unable to enter the new market and it is usually SMEs/DBFs that create new niches which later become new sectors. In order to survive, the SME/DBF must eventually become a vertically integrated producer. It needs to have a clear development strategy, aimed at creating, producing and marketing its own products. This implies that the firm will have to grow very rapidly in order to integrate vertically and to acquire the complementary assets required in addition to its existing scientific and technological skills.
- Second, the SME/DBF can attempt to exploit a *small and very specialized niche*. Such a niche would differ from that established by a Schumpeterian innovator: the former would remain small, while the latter could grow into a large market. Such a specialized niche would not be of great interest for large firms.

- Third, the SME/DBF could be a *supplier of knowledge services*. In a general sense the SME/DBF would explore the scientific and technological environment, either by conducting contract research or through technological collaboration with large firms and other partners. In this role the SME/DBF would not become vertically integrated.

An SME/DBF can play several of these roles simultaneously or in a sequence. For example, even an SME/DBF which intends to become vertically integrated may need, in the meantime, to be a supplier of knowledge services. More importantly, the roles played by SMEs/DBFs may differ depending on the country, the phase of the technology life cycle, and the particular biotechnology-based industrial sector. Thus the role of a Schumpeterian innovator is more likely in a country which is the first in establishing a technology (the US in biotechnology) than in a country which imitates or develops discoveries made elsewhere. On the other hand, new entrants have been relatively less successful in the seeds industry, where incumbent firms maintained their control, even when the new entrants were experienced LDFs (Joly and Ducos, 1993).

Considering the advantages that DBFs/SMEs can have, it raises questions about whether pre-existing LDFs will be able to survive at all in biotechnology-based industries. Survival can be based on the combination of competences and assets which an LDF needs in order to compete effectively in the pharmaceutical, chemical, agro-food and other sectors which can be influenced by biotechnology. The competences and assets required in addition to scientific and technological ones are, for example, marketing, legal and financial. Even if we consider scientific and technological competences as the core competences (Prahalad and Hamel, 1990) of a biotechnology-based firm, other competences, which Teece (1986) calls complementary assets, are required in order to produce and sell products. This is particularly the case if the new technology leads to changes in process technology, as was the case for biotechnology at the beginning. For example, the competences involved in the approval procedures for a new pharmaceutical product are the same as those required for an existing one, and it takes a long time for new entrants to acquire these competences. Moreover, what is crucial is not just the acquisition of these assets, but their integration within an organization. It must be noted that LDFs could survive with a level of knowledge which is less detailed and specific than that of DBFs in particular niches. In order for an LDF to survive economically it must have a level of scientific knowledge in molecular biology and in the other disciplines underpinning biotechnology which, *combined* with other complementary assets and competences, can allow it to deliver the final applications. In other words, the crucial capability of an LDF as compared with SMEs/DBFs in biotechnology-based sectors is to integrate different forms of knowledge, competences and assets. The relative stability of SMEs/DBFs and of LDFs, then, does not have to be judged in terms of a choice between the former and the latter. It is quite possible for each of them to have comparative advantages which would allow their simultaneous and perhaps symbiotic survival. Thus SMEs/DBFs can be expected to be in an advantageous position to exploit speed and depth of learning in specific areas. On the other hand, LDFs would have comparative advantages in scale economies and in the ability to integrate different competences and assets. The advantages due to scale economies would imply that LDFs have an incentive to concentrate on fewer, larger projects. This would leave a complementary role for SMEs/DBFs, that of rapidly scanning emerging fields of knowledge which, because of their newness, are still narrow and imperfectly structured. An SME/DBF could act as a sensor and a link between public research laboratories and LDFs. The comparative advantage in integrating different forms of knowledge and competences implies that an LDF could survive even by integrating externally generated knowledge. Of course, the LDF must have a sufficient absorption capacity in order to be able to achieve this integration. The construction of an absorption capacity implies that the LDF itself has to carry out some R&D in the fields which it wants to absorb. However, the level of knowledge acquired in these fields must not necessarily be equal to that of an SME/DBF. In this situation we can foresee a high degree of complementarity between SMEs/DBFs and LDFs, at least for a considerable period of time. For example, a possible role hypothesized for SMEs/DBFs is that of knowledge intermediaries between public research centres and LDFs (Figure 3.2). Route No. 1 could be replaced by a combination of Route Nos. 2 and 3. An LDF could have a gradual and incomplete learning in biotechnology while using some SMEs/DBFs as explorers and intermediaries in knowledge acquisition. Such a role for SMEs/DBFs would only lose its significance if new developments in the knowledge underlying biotechnology were to slow down, thus allowing LDFs to catch up completely and to outperform SMEs/DBFs through their integration capabilities. The probability of such a scenario taking place in the short to medium term is discussed in the following section on inter-firm collaborative agreements and networks.

Given the difficulty of acquiring and integrating different types of knowledge, competences and assets at their foundation, most SMEs/DBFs were forced to exploit their comparative advantage – the easy access to the new biotechnological knowledge – and did not integrate vertically. This involved carrying out contract research or entering into technological alliances with LDFs, as demonstrated even in the case of a

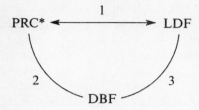

Note: PRC = public research centre.

Figure 3.2 The role of SMEs/DBFs as knowledge intermediaries

firm with a clear strategy for long-term vertical integration such as Genentech (McKelvey, 1994). During the 1980s the relationship between SMEs/DBFs and LDFs was one of complementarity. Even at the end of the 1980s very few SMEs/DBFs had managed to become completely vertically integrated, moving from R&D to taking products to market (Grabowsky and Vernon, 1994), even though some degree of integration, for example into production, now seems to be taking place in the US (Pisano, 1991). In spite of the very important role played by SMEs/DBFs, they are not replacing LDFs as suppliers of biotechnology-based products. What seems to have emerged, both in the US and in Europe, is an industrial structure characterized by a high degree of complementarity between SMEs/DBFs and LDFs. A very important question is whether such an industrial structure is likely to be stable in the future or whether it is only temporary. If we assume that the barrier faced by LDFs in entering biotechnology-based industries is due only to the difficulty of accessing the new knowledge, and if such new knowledge once established does not change very quickly, then we might expect the comparative advantage of the SMEs/DBFs to be gradually eroded by learning taking place in LDFs. There is evidence that by the end of the 1980s some LDFs in the US were acquiring the ability to incorporate biotechnology (Grabowsky and Vernon, 1994). If this were the case we could hypothesize a long-term industrial structure in which SMEs/DBFs, after having exerted a fundamental influence on the establishment of biotechnology-based industries, would disappear, leaving only LDFs. If, however, knowledge continues to develop at a very rapid pace, the comparative advantage of the SMEs/DBFs in searching and exploring new knowledge, even if on behalf of LDFs, would survive in the long term. At the moment it seems quite difficult to give a definitive answer to this question, even if the present industrial structure seems to be characterized by a high degree of complementarity between SMEs/DBFs and

LDFs. The high rate of diffusion of IICAs, which started in the early 1980s, seems to indicate, among other things, that mechanisms of knowledge creation, accumulation and use are changing and leading to more flexible industrial structures.

INTER-FIRM COLLABORATIVE AGREEMENTS

Until the 1980s inter-firm collaborative agreements tended to occur mostly in relation to technology transfer between firms in developed and developing countries. In developed countries IICAs were regarded as an unstable and inefficient form of industrial organization, compared with either markets or hierarchical organizations. Starting from the beginning of the 1980s the frequency of IICAs increased sharply (Chesnais, 1988; Hagedoorn and Schakenraad, 1990, 1992; Mytelka, 1991; Senker and Sharp, 1997). These IICAs were not only more frequent, but qualitatively different with respect to the previous ones. For example, new IICAs were often concerned with the creation of new knowledge, while old IICAs were used to transfer existing knowledge between developed and developing countries' firms. Moreover, new IICAs are often, even if not always, between actual or potential competitors (Amin, 1996). IICAs are particularly frequent in the so-called high technology sectors, such as IT, biotechnology or new materials. A number of studies have appeared about the motivations for, and mechanism of, IICAs. A number of factors have been mentioned as possible causes for the increased frequency of IICAs. The most general explanation points towards the increased uncertainty of the environment in which firms operate, due, for example, to globalization, increased competitiveness and the very rapid pace of technological change. In biotechnology, the continuing advances at the technological frontier justify the preservation of SMEs/DBFs as intermediaries in knowledge generation and utilization between public research centres and LDFs. For example, once scarce recombinant DNA techniques have now become part of the undergraduate curriculum and have been replaced as leading-edge technologies by polymerase chain reaction, gene sequencing and protein engineering (Senker and Sharp, 1997). SMEs/DBFs and LDFs continue to have complementary assets, which is one of the leading reasons for inter-firm collaboration. According to Senker and Sharp, the reasons for collaborating can be classified as: (1) the presence of complementary assets in SMEs/DBFs and in LDFs; (2) the close interaction and learning required for the exchange of such complementary assets; (3) the rapid scientific/technological advance which puts a premium on speed of learning; (4) the importance of preserving flexibility or reversibility of decisions; and (5) the need for trust. That complementary assets are a factor leading to IICAs has been pointed out by a number of other studies (see, for example, Arora and Gambardella, 1990; Pisano, 1991; Forrest and Martin, 1992; Ahern, 1993). Such causes can be of variable importance depending on the type of IICA and on the external environment in which firms operate. For example, links with universities play a different role for DBFs than their links with LDFs. Thus different types of partners satisfy different functions. Furthermore, strategic alliances are not independent of each other. Arora and Gambardella (1990) found evidence of complementarity between different strategic alliances. The changing nature of the environment can affect the significance of the speed of learning. Speed of learning is likely to be particularly important in times of radical, competence-destroying technological change, but to lose importance progressively when technological change becomes more incremental. A number of observations show that the nature of IICAs has changed over time. For example, according to Senker and Sharp (1997) LDFs' use of IICAs went through three specific phases: (1) a contract research phase, when firms were still very uncertain about developments; (2) a source of skills/recruitment/takeover phase; and (3) a source of new products/licensing for development phase. Also, according to Grabowsky and Vernon (1994), while DBFs continue to play a very significant role as intermediaries in knowledge generation and utilization, a number of LDFs have internalized biotechnology to a very significant extent. According to Bullock and Dibner (1995), IICAs in the US no longer involve only LDFs and DBFs, and there has been a systematic development of forms of collaboration between DBFs. Håkansson, Kjellberg and Lundgren (1993) distinguish three dimensions of strategic alliance: the production base, the market base and the knowledge base. Furthermore, they suggest that various types of alliance are entered into in order to strengthen or broaden specific dimensions. The authors of this study find that firms tend to broaden their production bases by having alliances with firms of a different size and strengthen their knowledge base by having alliances with firms active in the same subject area.

The literature presented in this section is but a small sample of a much larger one, indicating both the importance and the changing nature of IICAs. The crucial question here is if and for how long IICAs will remain a fundamental component of the industrial structure of the biotechnology-based industries and of other high technology sectors. From a theoretical point of view, to the extent that IICAs are a response to the high environmental uncertainty created by radically new technologies, a decline in their frequency and importance could be predicted as the technology matures and begins to undergo more incremental types of change. Pisano

(1991), in spite of recognizing the importance of IICAs, maintains that there is evidence of a growing importance of the integration of new knowledge and of vertical integration by the LDFs in biotechnology. Also, as already mentioned, Grabowsky and Vernon (1994) found evidence of biotechnology learning by LDFs. There is always the possibility that SMEs/DBFs will grow to become vertically integrated producers, but the existing evidence suggests that this phenomenon will not be a general route for the disappearance of SMEs/DBFs. Continuing advances at the scientific frontier and the need to learn quickly while preserving flexibility and reversibility should ensure that the role of SMEs/DBFs in the industrial structure of the biotechnology-based industries will continue to be important in the foreseeable future.

NETWORKS OF COLLABORATION IN BIOTECHNOLOGY

The analysis of IICAs can be given a greater degree of realism and precision by means of the concept of network and network analysis techniques. It must be pointed out that the literature on networks is highly fragmented and that it is not the aim of this study to provide a synthesis of such literature. The literature on networks has instead been used selectively for the purposes of our study. Thus a network is considered to be a collection of agents (firms, public research centres and so on) connected by a series of links of different intensity and quality. A detailed analysis of the networks formed by US and European biotechnology firms is contained in Chapters 5 and 6. Without anticipating the results of the analysis of those chapters, we outline here the expected relationships between networks, traditional concepts of industrial organization, and the dynamics of knowledge creation and accumulation.

We have previously pointed out that economic theory lacks a ready explanation for the sudden diffusion and stability of IICAs. Unless IICAs are strictly bilateral, network concepts and techniques are a mode of analysis that is very well adapted to IICAs, because IICAs are a form of network. However, it must be recognized that network theory is not yet endowed with both internal coherence and compatibility with general economic theory. In spite of these limitations, however, network concepts and techniques provide us with very powerful analytical tools to study IICAs.

Several aspects of IICAs can be studied by means of networks. For example, the actors forming a network are by no means equal: some of them are far more crucial than others. This difference in importance is reflected, for example, by their degree of centrality: central actors are unavoidable partners in most networks while peripheral actors have only limited participation. If we combine this varying importance with the possibility of increasing returns to adoption in particular technologies, we can expect that prime-mover advantages will be significant in the formation of networks and that actors entering late will not necessarily be able to catch up. This would justify some of the preoccupation about the late entry of European firms in biotechnology and about the limited number and reduced role of SMEs/DBFs in Europe. Moreover, the density of a network measures the extent to which actors form links among themselves.

The previous analysis of the lags and other disadvantages of European firms in biotechnology suggests that networks of collaboration are likely to be asymmetrically developed in Europe and the US. In particular, the almost exclusive reliance of European LDFs on American DBFs for knowledge inputs is likely to determine highly asymmetric networks, with European ones being much more oriented towards the US than their American counterparts are towards Europe.

Links between actors vary not only in their intensity and asymmetry, but also in their quality. For example, the link between a DBF and a public research institution is by no means equivalent to that between the same DBF and a venture capital unit. Accordingly, networks can be classified on the basis of their predominant type of link (for example, scientific, financial, and so on).

In addition to these considerations, which relate mostly to static aspects, the development of networks can have interesting dynamic aspects. Thus we can expect density to increase with time and some networks to stabilize while others remain fluid. Even within stabilized networks the role of participants can change over the course of time.

Questions about the temporary or permanent character of IICAs can be reformulated in terms of networks. Are networks likely to survive if and as biotechnology matures and if innovation within it becomes more incremental and predictable? Alternatively, should we expect a disappearance of networks and a return to markets and to hierarchical organizations? Once again it must be stressed that the answer to this question is closely related to the dynamics of knowledge creation and accumulation. To the extent that such dynamics play creating and sustaining roles that are neither 'doable' by, or nor convenient for, LDFs, SMEs/DBFs and public research institutions will persist and form networks. As a final comment it must be said that even if networks were to stabilize we could not expect them to have the same degree of rigidity as hierarchical organizations.

THE LOCATION OF BIOTECHNOLOGY-BASED FIRMS

In a sense most studies of biotechnology in Europe are concerned with a question of location. Why did biotechnology arise exclusively in the US? In this sense the question could be reduced to the analysis of a series of factors which were present in the US but absent in Europe. Scientific capabilities in molecular biology in the mid 1970s were largely concentrated in the US. Likewise, venture capital units capable and willing – unlike banks – to provide financial capital to emerging DBFs, were originally a uniquely American phenomenon. Location issues could thus be reduced to a list of factors which had facilitated the commercialization of biotechnology in the US. Policies arising from this analysis would aim to replicate the significant factors in areas where it was wished to establish biotechnology firms. However, such analysis requires considerably more subtlety. First, the 'factors' are not independent of the context in which they have developed and may not be portable. Neither scientific and technological competences in molecular biology and genetic engineering, nor venture capital units, developed in the US purely by accident. They are partly related to features of the economic and social environment of that country, and such features are not easily reproducible elsewhere. Furthermore, there is a more detailed structure underlying the issue of location. The possibility of increasing returns to establishing productive activities in a certain place can lead to economies of agglomeration, a possibility envisaged long ago by Marshall (1920) and revived recently in the literature on industrial districts, and on increasing returns (Arthur, 1989; Krugman, 1991). Concerning knowledge generation in particular, the source of increasing returns is spillovers or knowledge externalities (see, for example, Jaffe, 1986; Jaffe, Trajtenberg and Henderson, 1993; Audretsch and Feldman, 1994). The problem then arises of whether such knowledge externalities are more easily exploited locally. Evidence seems to indicate that this is indeed the case (Jaffe, Trajtenberg and Henderson, 1993), even though the extent of localization seems to decrease with time and when the roles played by biotechnology experts are not all equally dependent on location (Audretsch and Stephan, 1994). The important policy implication following from this discussion is the need to establish biotechnology firms and research centres in close proximity, as, for example, in a science park.

THE EXPERIENCE OF SOME EUROPEAN COUNTRIES

The experience of European countries cannot be analysed in isolation from that of the US. Biotechnology firms started emerging in America in the second half of the 1970s, initially in the form of DBFs. The pioneering role of US DBFs was probably linked to the development of molecular biology and genetic engineering in that country. At the beginning of the 1980s the influence of biotechnology DBFs on the pharmaceutical industry was very important. Most of the biopharmaceuticals approved for the US market originated in DBFs (Grabowsky and Vernon, 1994). However, established pharmaceutical firms also began to adopt biotechnology from the beginning of the 1980s. The result of this complex pattern of entry was that the industrial and innovative concentration of the pharmaceutical industry fell throughout the 1980s (Grabowsky and Vernon, 1994). In spite of their great importance, it is rare for DBFs to become vertically integrated producers. A more typical role for DBFs is that of suppliers of knowledge services, for example as R&D contractors and through technological alliances. In this sense the role of the typical DBF has been, and continues to be, complementary to that of the LDFs.

The number of DBFs in the US grew until the second half of the 1980s and then peaked at about the present number (approximately 950). Health care (therapeutics, diagnostics, vaccines) still constitutes the largest segment, followed by agricultural biotechnology. Important changes are expected to take place in the health care segment because the estimated growth of US sales of biotechnology-based drugs does not seem adequate to support all the current DBFs. Failures, mergers and concentrations are expected to take place in greater numbers over the next five years. Strong growth is expected in the food/agriculture area and possibly in environmental biotechnology (Bullock and Dibner, 1995).

European SMEs/DBFs were slow to emerge, and there are many less of them than in the US (see, for example, Escourrou, 1992; Walsh, Niosi and Mustar, 1995; Senker and Sharp, 1997). Within Europe, Britain has the largest number of SMEs/DBFs, followed by France, Germany and Sweden or the Netherlands (Escourrou, 1992; Ernst & Young, 1996). Almost all the factors that were considered to be important in determining the entry of DBFs were present in much smaller concentrations in Europe than in the US. Thus at least until the mid 1980s, scientific and technological capabilities in biotechnology in Europe were very limited, as shown, for example, by the share of publications and patents in bioengineering and in genetic engineering (Orsenigo, 1989, pp. 65–9). It took several public programmes (see Chapter 2) to improve the situation.

Government programmes in European countries are generally intended to remedy the lack of some of the factors that occur spontaneously in the US. In addition to scientific and technological capabilities, venture capital is considered an important factor. Venture capital availability in European countries is considerably smaller than that in the US (Walsh, Niosi and Mustar, 1995), although some recent developments seem to have partly bridged the gap. On the other hand, there is evidence that self-generated profits seem to be more important than contributions from venture capital firms (Walsh, Niosi and Mustar, 1995, Ernst & Young, 1995).

SUMMARY AND CONCLUSIONS

In this chapter we have analysed the factors considered to be important determinants of the industrial structure now prevalent in the biotechnology-based industries. Such industrial structure is constituted by a combination of LDFs and SMEs, in particular those which have been founded specifically either to carry out R&D or to produce new biotechnology-based products (DBFs). Moreover, an important role is played in the biotechnology-based industries by IICAs between LDFs, SMEs/DBFs and public research institutions. While the same types of actor can be found in the biotechnology-based industries in all countries studied, their relative roles vary widely. In particular, SMEs/DBFs are present in smaller numbers and play a much more limited role in European countries than in the US.

In this chapter we have also examined the factors that determine entry into the biotechnology-based industries. Profitability, regulation and venture capital are factors mentioned systematically in all studies on the economic development of biotechnology. Furthermore, the dynamics of knowledge creation and use can play a particularly important role in biotechnology. Modern biotechnology is based on developments in molecular biology and genetic engineering, which represent a radical departure from the knowledge previously used by firms. Such discontinuity creates conditions that are particularly favourable to new entrants. However, new entrants do not substitute for pre-existing firms, but play new roles, such as intermediaries in knowledge between LDFs and public research institutions or explorers. SMEs/DBFs play these and other roles not in isolation, but as part of an integrated industrial structure in which LDFs, public research institutions and SMEs/DBFs are linked by IICAs. To the extent that SMEs/DBFs play a fundamental role in the development of the biotechnology-based industries, their limited presence can constitute a source of weakness for European countries. The analysis conducted at a general level in this chapter is developed in much greater detail in Chapters 5 and 6, where the knowledge base and the networks formed by European SMEs/DBFs are examined.

REFERENCES

Ahern, R. (1993), 'Implications of strategic alliances for small R&D-intensive firms', *Environment and Planning A*, **25**(10), 1511–26.

Amin, M. (1996), 'Understanding "strategic alliances": the limit of transaction cost economics', in R. Coombs, A. Richards, P. Saviotti and V. Walsh (eds), *Technological Collaboration: The Dynamics of Co-operation in Industrial Innovation*, Aldershot: Edward Elgar, pp.165–79.

Arora, A. and A. Gambardella (1990), 'Complementarity and external linkages: the strategies of the large firms in biotechnology', *Journal of Industrial Economics*, **38**(4), 361–79.

Arthur, W.B. (1989), *Silicon Valley Locational Clusters: When Do Increasing Returns Imply Monopoly?*, Working Paper 89-007, Santa Fe Institute.

Audretsch, D.B. (1995), *Innovation and Industry Evolution*, Cambridge, MA: MIT Press.

Audretsch, D.B. and M.P. Feldman (1994), *R&D Spillovers and the Geography of Innovation and Production*, Berlin: Wissenschaftzentrum Berlin für Sozialforschung (WZB), Working Paper.

Audretsch, D.B. and P. Stephan (1994), *Company Scientists' Locational Links: The Case of Biotechnology*, Mimeo, Berlin: Wissenschaftzentrum Berlin für Sozialforschung and Palo Alto: Center for Economic Policy Research, Stanford University, CA.

Bullock, W.O. and M.D. Dibner (1995), 'The state of the US biotechnology industry', *TIBTECH*, **13**, 463–7.

Chesnais, F. (1988), 'Technical cooperation agreement between independent firms, novel issues for economic analysis and the formulation of national technological policies', *STI Review*, No. 4, 51–120.

Chesnais, F. and V. Walsh (1994), *Biotechnology and the Chemical Industry: The Relevance of Some Evolutionary Concepts*, paper presented at the EUNETIC Conference, Strasbourg, 6–8 October.

Cohen, M. and D. Levinthal (1989), 'Innovation and learning: the two faces of R&D', *Economic Journal*, **99**(397), 569–96.

Cohen, M. and D. Levinthal (1990), 'Absorptive capacity: a new perspective on learning and innovation', *Administrative Science Quarterly*, **35**(1), 128–52.

De Looze, M.A., J. Estades, P.B. Joly, S. Ramani, P.P. Saviotti, J. Senker and J.L. Pedersen (1996), *The Role of SMEs/DBFs in Technology Creation and Diffusion: Implications for European Competitiveness in Biotechnology*. A report for the European Commission, CT-942032, Grenoble: INRA-SERD.

Ernst & Young (1995), *European Biotech 95. Gathering Momentum*, London: Ernst & Young International.

Ernst & Young (1996), *European Biotech 96. Volatility and Value*, London: Ernst & Young International.

Escourrou, N. (1992), 'Les societés de biotechnologie européennes: un réseau très imbriqué', *Biofutur*, July–August, 40–2.

Forrest, J.E. and J.C. Martin (1992), 'Strategic alliances between large and small research intensive organizations: experiences in the biotechnology industry', *R&D Management*, **22**(1), 41–53.

Gort, M. and S. Klepper (1982), 'Time paths in the diffusion of product innovations', *Economic Journal*, **92**(367), 630–53.

Grabowsky, H. and J. Vernon (1994), 'Innovation and structural change in pharmaceuticals and biotechnology', *Industrial and Corporate Change*, **3**(2), 435–49.

Hagedoorn, J. and J. Schakenraad (1990), 'Inter-firm partnerships and cooperative strategies in core technologies', in C. Freeman and L. Soete (eds), *New Explorations in the Economics of Technological Change*, London: Pinter Publishers.

Hagedoorn, J. and J. Schakenraad (1992), 'Intercompany cooperation and technological developments – leading companies and networks of strategic alliances in information technologies', *Research Policy*, **21**(2), 163–90.

Håkansson, P., H. Kjellberg and A. Lundgren (1993), 'Strategic alliances in global biotechnology – a network approach', *International Business Review*, **2**, 65–82.

Henderson, R.M. (1993), 'Underinvestment and incompetence as responses to radical innovation – evidence from the photolithographic alignment equipment industry', *Rand Journal of Economics*, **24**(2), 248–70.

Jaffe, A.B. (1986), 'Technological opportunities and spillovers of R&D: evidence from the firms' patents, profits and market value', *American Economic Review*, **76**, 984–1001.

Jaffe, A.B., M. Trajtenberg and R. Henderson (1993), 'Geographic localization of knowledge spillovers as evidenced by patent citations', *Quarterly Journal of Economics*, **100**(3), 577-98.

Joly, P.B. and C. Ducos (1993), *Les Artifices du Vivant: Stratégies d'Innovation dans l'Industrie des Semences*, Paris: INRA-Economica.

Kenney, M. (1986), *Biotechnology: The University–Industry Complex*, New Haven, Conn.: Yale University Press.

Krugman, P. (1991), *Geography and Trade*, Cambridge, MA: MIT Press.

Liebeskind, J.P., A.L. Oliver, L.G. Zucker and M.B. Brewer (1995), *Social Networks, Learning and Flexibility: Sourcing Scientific Knowledge in New Biotechnology Firms*, NBER Working Paper 5320, Cambridge, MA.: National Bureau of Economic Research.

Marshall, A. (1920), *Principles of Economics*, 8th Edition, London: Macmillan.

McCain, K.W. (1995), 'The structure of biotechnology R&D', *Scientometrics*, **32**(2), 153–75.

McKelvey, M. (1994), *Evolutionary Innovation: Early Industrial Uses of Genetic Engineering*, S-581 83, Linköping, Sweden: Department of Technology and Social Change, Linköping University.

Mytelka, L.K. (ed.) (1991), *Strategic Partnership and the World Economy*, London: Pinter Publishers.

Oakey, R., W. Faulkner, S. Cooper and V. Walsh (1990), *New Firms in the Biotechnology Industry*, London: Pinter Publishers.

Orsenigo, L. (1989), *The Emergence of Biotechnology: Institutions and Markets in Industrial Innovation*, London: Pinter Publishers.

Pisano, G. (1991), 'The governance of innovation: vertical integration and collaborative arrangements in the biotechnology industry', *Research Policy*, **20**(3), 237–49.

Prahalad, C.K. and G. Hamel (1990), 'The core competence of the corporation', *Harvard Business Review*, May–June, 79–91.

Rip, A. and L. Courtial (1984), 'Co-word maps of biotechnology: an example of cognitive scientometrics', *Scientometrics*, **6**(6), 381–400.

Saviotti, P.P. (1996), *Technological Evolution, Variety and the Economy*, Aldershot: Edward Elgar.

Schumpeter, J.A. (1912), *The Theory of Economic Development*, reprinted (1934), Cambridge, MA: Harvard University Press.

Senker, J. (1996), 'National systems of innovation, organizational learning and industrial biotechnology', *Technovation*, **16**(5), 219–29.

Senker, J., P.-B. Joly and M. Reinhard (1996), *Overseas Biotechnology Research by Europe's Chemical/Pharmaceuticals Multinationals: Rationale and Implications*, Final Report for the Biotechnology Programme (BIOTECH) of the European Community, DG XII, STEEP Discussion Paper No. 33, Brighton: Science Policy Research Unit, University of Sussex.

Senker, J. and M. Sharp (1997), 'Organisational learning in cooperative alliances: some case studies in biotechnology', *Technology Analysis & Strategic Management*, **9**(1), 35–51.

Teece, D. (1986), 'Profiting from technological innovation', *Research Policy*, **15**(6), 285–305.

Tushman, M.L. and P. Anderson (1986), 'Technological discontinuities and organizational environments', *Administrative Science Quarterly*, **31**(3), 439–65.

Walsh, V., J. Niosi and P. Mustar (1995), 'Small firm formation in biotechnology: a comparison of France, Britain and Canada', *Technovation*, **15**(5), 303–27.

Winter, S.G. (1984), 'Schumpeterian competition in alternative technological regimes', *Journal of Economic Behaviour and Organizations*, **5**(3–4), 287–320.

4. Risk perception, regulation and the management of agro-biotechnologies

Joanna Chataway and **Gerald Assouline**

INTRODUCTION

Risk regulation and the way in which risk is perceived and managed are emerging as key factors in competitiveness. The recent very high profile controversy over 'mad cow disease' and the dangers it poses to humans, for example, has put risk very much at the centre of public debate. This chapter summarizes some of the principal findings from a research project studying attempts to manage risk regulation and risk perception of agro-biotechnologies in the European Union (EU).[1] The study looked at the UK, France and the Netherlands,[2] and included extensive interviews with over 60 industrialists, regulators and non-governmental organizations (NGOs).

The research examined the main factors influencing the debate about risk regulation and the different ways in which risk regulation and perception are managed. We looked at industry strategies, regulators' attitudes, mechanisms for avoiding damage to the environment and health, and NGOs' activities. The study focused on herbicide resistance and biopesticides, but has more general implications for the deliberate release of genetically modified organisms (GMOs). More conceptual points made in the chapter also have implications for medical applications of biotechnology.

The study was broad and this chapter does not attempt to summarize all aspects of the project. We do not provide detail about specific national contexts here, and a great deal of the information and analysis which we carried out on regulators' and NGOs' views is not discussed. Rather, we have attempted to provide an overview of the way in which the debate is moving and we have focused on industry's position with regard to risk regulation.

Concern about Europe's competitiveness in biotechnology and the possible negative effects of stringent regulations on the one hand and anxiety about the environmental consequences of releasing GMOs on the other, make the debate about regulation controversial and often bitter. Recent discussion indicates that in some contexts, at least, there is a new willingness from interested parties in industry, NGOs and regulators to try and create shared ground. However, there is still widespread disagreement about the nature of risk regulation and the innovations themselves. In the case of NGOs, a division now exists between those willing to discuss the detail of deliberate release and labelling regulation and those who oppose all release of genetically altered products on the grounds that no regulation can guarantee against damage to the environment and health, and any risk is too great a risk.

The focal point of the debate has moved from controversy over whether deliberate release regulation should be vertical or horizontal to discussion about the remit of regulation. Also, as more products come closer to market, companies are worrying more about risk perception and issues to do with labelling, and are less concerned about pushing for deregulation.

Disagreement about risk management to some extent reflects differences in the way that regulators, companies and NGOs think about uncertainty. This chapter discusses technocratic and adaptive strategies for coping with uncertainty and relates them to the risk debate. We also explore differences within industry's approach to risk regulation and perception, outlining a typology of strategies and providing some examples of the different ways in which companies manage risk. While this research focuses on agriculture and food-related biotechnology, regulation and perception of risk also need careful management in the area of pharmaceuticals and health care. The chapter comments briefly on implications for this sector.

RISK REGULATION AT THE EUROPEAN LEVEL AND THE CONTEXT IN WHICH INNOVATION TAKES PLACE

The Current Regulatory Framework

The use, manufacture, release and marketing of GMOs are now governed by two principal regulations: the Genetically Modified Organisms (contained use) Regulations 1992 (90/219) and the Genetically Modified Organisms (deliberate release) Regulations 1992 (90/220). Deliberate release regulations apply to GMOs released into the environment – for example, field testing – or placed for sale on the market. Both contained and deliberate release regulations apply only to viable organisms (organisms which can replicate themselves). These regulations implement the two European Community directives on contained and deliberate release.

There is some pressure from industry for a substantial revision of 90/219 in order to make the procedures easier to deal with. Industry claims that the regulations cause significant delay and have negative consequences for competitiveness. It is likely that there will be pressure to revise 90/219 in the current review of procedures. However, this directive is not subject to high profile discussion in the way that 90/220 has been.

Many industry managers and analysts have in the past been very vocal in their opposition to the directive on deliberate release, as evidenced by documents produced by the Senior Advisory Group on Biotechnology (SAGB, 1990) and a number of industry submissions to the House of Lords 1993 inquiry (House of Lords, 1993). There does now seem to be increasing acceptance from industry that the regulations in their present form, including 'fast track' procedures for planned releases which have been examined in the past, are acceptable.

This is certainly not to say that debates about risk regulation are over. Rather, the terrain seems to be shifting. Whereas industry in the past framed the debate with high profile calls for deregulation, the debate now tends to focus on forms of regulation and the management of the regulatory process. Much has been written about the consequences and implications of 'process-based' or 'horizontal' regulations on which the directives were modelled (Tait and Levidow, 1992; Chataway and Tait, 1993; Shohet, 1996).[3] We shall not attempt to summarize the debate in full. The following section outlines some key aspects of the main debate about risk and discusses the context in which the debate takes place. In order to understand the debate and the implications of decisions made about how to manage risk regulation and perception, attention must be given to the broader environment.

The Broad Debate about Risk

Risk now occupies a central place in debates about a number of new technologies. For some risk is viewed as a purely 'scientific' question which can be addressed in technical terms. Increasingly, however, risk is seen as a social phenomenon, properly subject to political debate and increasingly demanding more active participation from relevant groups. If definitions of risk are accepted as socially and politically defined, rather than objective realities, risk perception becomes a key issue. Risk regulation cannot be viewed as a technical undertaking, but rather a negotiated set of rules which try to balance competing social interests. This view of risk regulation derives in part from a particular view of uncertainty and how it is best coped with. Acha comments that risk and uncertainty are often viewed as the same thing. She says:

> They are not the same thing. According to the *Concise Oxford Dictionary* (eighth edition), to be uncertain is to be 'not certainly knowing or known' or 'unreliable' or 'changeable, erratic' (as in the case of the weather). All of these definitions imply a concern about facing the unforeseen. This is often described in terms of a 'risk' that things will not turn out as planned ... To sum up, uncertainty is the state of not knowing; risk is our assessment of what may happen under a state of uncertainty. (Acha, 1997, p.5)

Table 4.1 outlines two different approaches to coping with uncertainty.

The broad debate about how risk regulation should be defined underlies the controversy over biotechnology regulation in that biotechnology has marked a new era in environmental risk regulation. EU regulation of GMO release has provoked bitter argument between industry, Commission directorates and pressure groups. Those who favour a technocratic approach to uncertainty tended towards strong opposition to the deliberate release directive as it was originally formulated.

The debate revolves around growing pressure to adopt increasingly proactive risk regulatory regimes, in contrast to the reactive risk regulations which operated in the 1950s, 60s and 70s. New products were assumed to be harmless until proved to be otherwise. Once a hazard had been identified, regulations were established so that new risks did not pose the same set of risks. No organized attempt was made to anticipate previously unforeseen hazards. In the case of biotechnology, an attempt was made to install proactive regulations. A proactive approach signifies an attempt to identify problems in advance of the development and distribution of products.

Proactive risk regimes force the issue of broader participation to an even greater degree; perception of risk does not necessarily correspond to quantitative assessment and this complicates the politics of regulation. The proactive approach requires public input into the regulatory process. Perceptions of risk, indeed the definition of risk, will in part depend on who is doing the perceiving.

These rather abstract notions of reactive and proactive regulation are intimately connected with a discussion about the merits of product-based and process-based regulatory regimes. Those who believe that GMOs pose no inherent risks favour product-based regulatory regimes based on existing regulatory structures. Others favour process-based regimes on the grounds that novel organisms may have unforeseen negative consequences for the environment. Proponents of process-based regimes tend to favour horizontal structures which have additional regulatory hurdles to monitor potential risks of GMOs. Those who favour product-based regimes

Table 4.1 Contrasting strategies for coping with uncertainty

Technocrat strategies

Principles	Efficiency		Control	
Techniques	Quantified risk analysis Limited experimentation		Centralization Reporting requirements and strict adherence to procedures	
	One policy route followed		Information management; collection at the planning stage and at completion	
	Standard procedures		Expectations management	

Adaptive strategies

Principles	Flexibility	Diversity	Compromise	Learning
Techniques	Stage the development of policy	Follow more than one policy route	Balance what is at risk with what is at stake	Prioritize information collection, analysis, dissemination
	Decentralize decision making	Experiment with policy strategies	Build consensus among: policy makers, beneficiaries, wider community	Provide incentives and the means to respond to them
	Avoid extremes, potential policy 'lock in'	Adapt models to specific conditions	Be open and encourage discussion among opposing interests	Learn continuously by monitoring and re-conceptualizing

Source: Acha 1997.

also advocate vertical structures on the grounds that any risks can effectively be monitored by systems set up to deal with foods, drugs and pesticides (with additional product-based channels for genetically manipulated plants).

POTENTIAL ENVIRONMENTAL RISKS OF GMOs

These larger, more conceptual debates are intertwined with discussions operating at a greater level of detail about concrete risks posed by GMO release into the environment. The conceptual issues tend at times to overshadow discussion of the more detailed risks. This is partly because the conceptual debates are more easily accessible to a wider range of people and partly because the debate about safety regulation has been confused with much broader debates about whether or not products of biotechnology are useful and the ethics of biotechnology.

As more releases have occurred over the 1980s and 90s, a number of key issues have formed the core of the debate about the concrete risks of GMO release. These are:

- *persistence*: the danger that GMOs will show unexpected competitive traits, become established and even become pests in natural and semi-natural environments;
- *danger to non-target organisms*: possible consumption of plants modified to express toxins by non-target organisms or humans;
- *horizontal spread of genes and ecological imbalance*: concern about the spread of toxins engineered into plants;
- *longer-term control problems*: the spread of herbicide resistance in modified crops to weeds, making their control more difficult. This could become a particular problem if a number of different herbicide-resistant products were used over a long period of time;
- *agronomic risk*: the build-up of resistance to products such as *Bacillus thuringiensis* (Bt) potentially leaves farmers vulnerable and undermines the model of high input agriculture.

At the level of microbial releases, additional issues arise:

- *altered virulence and widening of host range*: the possibility of the genetic modification of viruses resulting in altered virulence or widening of the host range;
- *natural resource disturbance*: possible alteration of nutrient and water cycles through genetic modification of the bacteria that play a key role in them.

It is predominantly around these issues that the scientific and technical argument takes place. Specific cases are judged to be more or less risky, and most involved in the debate accept that with appropriate testing and monitoring, risks are to a large extent definable, although of course there is still disagreement about what constitutes appropriate testing and monitoring. For example, should risk regulation concern itself with the way in which products are used? Where should the boundaries defining risk regulation be placed? Should risk regulation be based on research to be conducted to determine the long-term impact of technologies? There is also debate as to what extent risk regulation should include additional socio-economic and ethical issues.

Industry, regulators and a number of NGOs participate in these debates. However, it is important to note that there are some NGOs which do not engage in these more detailed debates. Greenpeace, for instance, objects to all deliberate release on the grounds that no matter the type of regulatory regime, tests will not be able to provide sufficient information about long-term impacts on health and the environment. This type of wholesale challenge and the issue of labelling are becoming focal points in the debate over genetic engineering.

The following are some of the key areas around which discussion of deliberate release regulation currently revolves:

Harmonization

Difficulties in furthering harmonization result from varied practices and differences of regulatory culture in Europe. While much of industry considers that a unified European regulatory structure would be beneficial, the reality is complex and countries appear to be a long way away from being willing, or perhaps even able, to implement one cohesive set of regulatory practices.

There are many detailed questions about harmonization which have yet to be addressed. These questions relate not only to regulatory mechanisms but also to the extent to which harmonized regulations will be perceived and viewed as legitimate.

Long-Term Monitoring

There are no standard procedures for long-term monitoring of the impact of release of genetically engineered organisms. Indeed there is no consensus that long-term monitoring is within the remit of regulatory authorities. This is an area in which there is likely to be more debate and where there may be room for further coordination between regulatory agencies in different countries. One of the key discussion areas concerns concrete identification of the areas on which long-term monitoring should focus and the questions which need to be asked.

Information

Countries pursue different practices for diffusion of information about deliberate releases. This is partially connected to varying levels of concern about release in different countries.

The way in which information is made available to the public is an important element of regulation. Efforts to improve access to information and to make the regulatory process more open are likely to enhance the perception of regulatory regimes. If there is to be further harmonization in regulation, this is an area requiring increased standardization.

Communication

Different companies and government agencies have attempted to facilitate communication about biotechnology and genetic engineering in a variety of ways. Consensus conferences, meetings organized by ministries responsible for regulation, and joint company and NGO workshops are all potentially powerful ways to promote dialogue about biotechnology. This becomes particularly important as more products of biotechnology reach the market.

As evaluations of consensus conferences and other methods of encouraging debate and dialogue are carried out, they are likely to generate more discussion about the usefulness of these types of event for different interest groups.

Labelling is not required for all products of biotechnology and this is emerging as a contentious issue. A number of NGOs and consumer groups are arguing that any product of genetic engineering must be labelled as such. Indeed there is a strategic alliance emerging among a wide range of NGOs and consumer groups around this issue. These groups differ over many aspects of biotechnology but are united around the demand for labelling of all genetically engineered products.

Boundaries around Risk Regulation

The boundaries of risk regulation are being questioned in a number of ways, some of which are apparent in previously mentioned points. 'Mad cow disease' and the very difficult communication issues which have faced regulatory authorities have highlighted questions around where risk regulation should begin and end. There is widespread disagreement among different European regulators on this issue, and among industry and

NGOs (Levidow et al., 1996). It has brought into question other aspects of 'technocratic' approaches to uncertainty and associated risk management strategies: for example, the belief that quantified risk analysis, standard procedures, one policy route and managed expectations should, and could, constitute the main tenents of a regulatory code.

Some companies and regulators still maintain that a 'technocratic' approach is the only viable set of regulatory procedures. Some NGOs respond with an equally adamant rejection of any GMO release. These NGOs can be thought of as inverting the technocratic approach and adopting it as their own: if quantifiable risk assessment cannot provide 100 per cent guarantee of zero risk, no releases should be allowed.

One of the main issues to do with risk regulation boundaries is the extent to which risk regulation should be concerned with the way in which products of biotechnology are used. For instance, one herbicide-resistant product may not pose any environmental risk if it is viewed in isolation, but the cumulative impact of different herbicide-resistant products may pose significant problems.

CONTEXTUAL FACTORS IN THE MANAGEMENT OF RISK REGULATION

The debate about risk regulation is best understood when examined within the context of the broader environment. This debate is in fact influenced by a number of factors and the context has changed in some significant ways since the mid 1980s.

First, there is intensive competitive pressure in contracting markets for the agricultural supply industry, pushing companies to accelerate product development, anticipate and provoke regulatory changes, and consolidate world-wide strategies. Second, growing evidence is emerging that food surpluses and 'food mountains', which led to policies such as set-aside, may shortly turn to food shortages. However, much of the infrastructure, a great deal of which was publicly funded, which supported technological innovation and led to increases in crop yield, has been dismantled. Third, added to this there is still a widespread perception that food production should be decreased rather than increased. The combination of these factors has meant that both private and public sectors have had enormous difficulty in formulating consistent strategies (Chataway and Tait, 1993).

A new heterogeneity of actors is emerging from industry and research who are building new kinds of alliances, partnerships and networks to cope with the complexity and diversity of techniques being mobilized. At the level of R&D, networks of small and large companies often work together to create new products. The growing pressures of competitiveness and a growing awareness of the power of consumer opinion has meant that new relationships throughout the supply chain, from chemical companies to retailers, need to be created. Public concerns about genetic engineering and biotechnology-derived food products give rise to public debates about environmental risk and food labelling. This has added to the complexity of developing new technologies and formulating strategy.

Regulators are finding it very difficult to develop public policies (national and supra-national) in the areas of agriculture and risk regulation which can be brought together to create an agreed framework for the development of biotechnology. Conflicting pressures – such as the need to cater for growing public concern about both chemical and biological inputs to agriculture while also ensuring that the quality and quantity of food production are maintained and creating an environment where production costs do not rise significantly – have led to increasing uncertainty about the nature of risk regulation and its relation to other forms of regulation, such as competition policy and broader agricultural policy.

COMPETITIVENESS AND INDUSTRY STRATEGIES

Industry Strategies

While the picture remains confused and companies are pursuing various avenues in the short term, the main priorities for biotechnology for most of the agro-chemical industry remain consolidation of the main activities and presence in core markets. Rather than develop totally new strategies based on new technological possibilities, such as developing biopesticides, multinationals have tended to target areas where they can combine chemical and biological inputs.

Agro-chemical multinationals' actions have to be considered with the following factors in mind:

- the cost of innovation is extremely high, which imposes some rigidities in companies' approach to innovation;
- some of the main actors in the area are heavily dominated by herbicide interests and so this strategy of consolidation makes sense both in financial terms and in making use of accumulated technical know-how (Chataway, 1992);
- companies are using genetic engineering to promote less environmentally damaging herbicides, thereby going some way towards complying with demands to reduce damage to the environment. Thus they can portray themselves as pursuing more environmentally friendly routes.

Food companies involved in biotechnology innovation have also been cautious about new developments. First, companies were sceptical about profit margins and worried that large R&D investments could not be recouped on food products. Second, food companies are fully aware of the power of consumer opinion and have been more actively involved than their agro-chemical counterparts in working with consumer and environmental groups to try and achieve a common understanding about the technology.

In the late 1980s and early 90s it seemed that many multinational companies thought they could win the battle over deregulation. Given the very difficult market situation, this was an important battle. There was a great deal of concern about investment in biotechnology and managers were keen to retain as much control over the innovation process as possible. Increasingly, given the focus on herbicide resistance and the dangers in terms of public relations of highlighting the revolutionary potential of biotechnology, managers were keen to emphasize the 'business as usual' aspects of the technology. Industry was convinced that awareness of specific risk regulation made people more, rather than less, worried about biotechnology innovations. In this context industry could maintain a united front, such as the front presented by the SAGB over the dangers of too much regulation in terms of competitiveness. This is changing, however.

There is evidence that industry is not trusted to tell the truth over regulation and that, contrary to the common view held in industry, people tend to have more, rather than less, confidence in the technology as a result of specific risk regulation (Kraus, 1994). Increasingly managers, especially in the food industry, are changing their attitudes to coping with uncertainty from those based on technocratic strategies to those based on adaptive strategies. At the same time, EU regulators have become more concerned with encouraging investment in biotechnology and are trying to streamline regulations so as not to deter investment. In some respects, then, the debate about risk regulation has become less polarized and more focused on the details of regulation and the communication around risk rather than on principles of deregulation. This more adaptive approach has opened up new areas of debate. However, in conjunction with, and partly because of, this trend, the debate has in other respects become more polarized. While some NGOs have been willing to engage in more detailed discussions about risk regulation, organizations such as Greenpeace are clearer about opposing all genetic engineering no matter which regulations are introduced. Also, as noted, some agro-chemical companies maintain their 'deregulationist' position.

The situation with regard to pharmaceuticals and health care applications of biotechnology is similar in some respects; the debate in this area has also changed and in part takes place at a greater level of detail than a decade ago. However, it is also the case that many different religious, NGO and other interest groups have serious ethical dilemmas over the development of certain biotechnology applications in this area and, again, ethical issues are dealt with in various ways by different European countries.

A large number of polls have been commissioned to try and gauge 'public opinion'. Many of these are of limited use because they do not give any indication of why people hold certain beliefs. However, a number of polls in Europe and the US indicate that gene therapy is seen as one of the most problematic biotechnology applications and that manipulation of human embryos is widely opposed in some areas of Europe (Zechendorf, 1994). It is very likely that attempts by industry to argue a strongly deregulationist and technocratic position will be strongly resisted. Ethical concerns and the value-laden nature of the debate mean that purely 'technocratic' approaches are unlikely to assuage concern about developments in this area. As regulators and industry try and grapple with more nebulous concerns, there are differing opinions about the impact of risk regulation on competitiveness.

Risk Regulation and Competitiveness

One of the most important debates underpinning current Commission policy is the gap which exists between Europe, the US and Japan. On this point, there has been clear agreement between the SAGB, the Commission and industry (Assouline and Chataway, 1995). The SAGB (1994, p. 5) and the Commission of the European Communities (1993) refer to several indicators which demonstrate the gap:

- the relatively small number of European patents for new biotechnology products granted around the world;
- the small proportion of biotechnology-based products currently marketed in Europe;
- the difficulties of marketing some products produced in Europe within the EU.

Factors which are currently considered as jeopardizing competitiveness in Europe include:

- the relative weakness of public R&D expenditure within the Community as compared with the US and Japan;
- the current 'horizontal/process-based' risk regulatory regime which deters innovation;

- hostility to biotechnology which is more pronounced in Europe than in the US and Japan.

This analysis leads the Commission (and SAGB) to advocate a broad range of policy initiatives, especially on regulatory questions (Table 4.2). Since the pro-biotechnology recommendations in the December 1993 White Paper on European competitiveness (Commission of the European Communities, 1993), the EU and member states have been working to develop a fast track for regulatory procedures.

Interestingly, the same kinds of argument are used in the US in order to modify and soften Environmental Protection Agency (EPA) and Food and Drug Administration (FDA) procedures. The Republican majority during the early 1990s pressured the FDA and EPA to modify their procedures. Environmental and consumer organizations strongly criticized the FDA's approach to reviewing genetically engineered foods. In fact, the FDA's biotechnology food policy is drawing criticism from numerous quarters, including some members of its own Food Advisory Committee.

There is a race between Europe and the US to grant marketing approval for genetically modified crops. In 1995, the French authorities gave marketing approval for a SEITA bromoxynil tolerant tobacco; this procedure confers EU-wide approval. Nevertheless, the immediate intention is not to market this tobacco but to conduct extensive testing. In

Table 4.2 Comparison of Commission and SAGB Recommendations

Common propositions	Specific recommendations	
Commission/SAGB	Commission	SAGB
More vertical regulation for GMOs (product-based)	Scientific Advisory body for Risk Assessment	Reduction of social costs
Support to small and medium-sized enterprises	Development of R&D programmes on focused areas	
Fiscal incentives	Coordinate and stimulate cooperation	
Training and mobility		

Source: Commission of the European Communities (1993), SAGB, (1994).

March 1995, the EPA gave a limited premarket registration to Ciba Seeds, Mycogen Plant Sciences and Monsanto, for the first stage of commercialization for pesticide-resistant corn, potato and cotton plants. These companies received the right to plant some 60 000 acres of engineered seeds in selected US states.

These examples suggest that regulation and marketing approval are used as instruments of competition between multinational companies which need to accelerate their product development and marketing. Regulators are also keen to maintain regulatory systems which constitute attractive environments for the development of biotechnology research and innovation capacity. It is this pressure to maintain competitive environments which has led to 'fast track' procedures and measures to make regulations more 'vertical'. However, within many companies views about the impact of risk regulation on competitiveness are more complex.

Management of Risk Regulation and Perception

Discussion about regulation and global competitiveness takes place at both the macro and micro level:

- on a macro level, national and supra-national authorities and industry argue that different regulatory systems can generate a 'gap' in competitiveness and encourage investment in the most conducive environments;
- on a micro level, inside the companies, regulation is not considered by many managers as a major hurdle to developing research and innovation capacities, which are the basis for competitive advantage. Risk regulation is seen as a strategic issue rather than a day-to-day managerial issue. For many managers, it is the concern that particular forms of risk regulation will have negative knock-on effects rather than worries about their direct impact. The issue is becoming how to manage risk regulation.

While the capacity to influence and anticipate the evolution of regulation is considered an important advantage in industrial competition, the most decisive factors for the development and competitiveness of research and innovation capacity in this instance, are not the regulatory ones. The world economic and political context, research and education policy, support to small and medium-sized firms, and the importance of perception of risk are just as important, or more important.

The way industry deals with public perception is not homogeneous and, indeed, is becoming more diverse. Differences in attitudes towards public opinion are very clearly seen in the food labelling debate, between consensual pro-labelling and firm non-labelling positions. Those who take a non-labelling position argue that labelling is costly and should not be required on products which have been through the regulatory process and have been deemed to pose no risk. High profile demonstrations against imports of labelled US GMO soybeans to Europe, however, are likely to have strengthened the stance taken by those who favour more 'adaptive' strategies and who are ready to negotiate types of labelling. In interviews, critics of the hard-line approaches tend to think that these strategies provoke inflexible responses and that in any case the impact of risk regulation on competitiveness may not be clear-cut.

Contributing Factors in Competitiveness

An Ernst & Young report entitled *European Biotechnology 95* documents that nearly four out of five respondents to an Ernst & Young survey said that EU directives have had no impact on their business. Only 15 per cent said they believed that the directives have had a negative impact (Ernst & Young, 1995). The survey included pharmaceutical companies and biotechnology companies focusing on medical applications.

A report written for the European Parliament (Kraus, 1994) discusses in detail the impact of environmental risk regulation on firms. The conclusion drawn in the report is that risk regulation does not constitute the main problem for the development of biotechnology in Europe. Other, more structural reasons explain the attraction of the US for large European companies and for the large population of dedicated biotechnology firms there. These include financial structures, knowledge infrastructure, research capacity and education, technology transfer and support to industry.

In the UK, the Centre for the Exploitation of Science and Technology tried to identify, rank and map the factors that influence scientific progress and successful commercial exploitation of plant biotechnology in the long term (Kidd and Dvorak, 1994). In general, the most compelling forces that can alter the future of agro-biotech are macroeconomic and political, rather than scientific- or product-related. These include the following structural factors:

- the world trade environment;
- political distortion of internal markets caused by subsidies;
- the viability of intensive and conventional farming;
- demographic and social changes.

There are other critical factors which have a meaningful impact on the future, but the degree to which they affect agro-biotech is hard to calculate. These include:

- human impact on the environment;
- the 'greening' of products and processes;
- public acceptance of agro-biotech.

Investment in science and current and anticipated return on investment indicate the future health and utility of agro-biotech. However, the following factors are thought to have a minimal impact on agro-biotech's future:

- advance in scientific knowledge;
- retailer promotion of biotech products;
- demand for differentiated farm products.

Obviously, this classification is not exhaustive and the factors which are thought to have minimal impact are perhaps surprising. Nevertheless, one distinction that can be drawn from the analysis is that some of those factors impacting on innovation are internal ones, that is, they can be controlled and modified by company management, while others are external to the company and need to be incorporated into strategic thinking. Of the factors which companies think affect the development of biotechnology, most are beyond their immediate control.

Risk perception falls into this latter category, although of course it is something over which companies can have influence. The main actors concerned by environmental risk perception are part of the agriculture supply industry, including pesticide and seed companies, and the more important biotechnology companies which are trying to push their products through to trials and commercialization (such as the company Plant Genetic Systems). They face several difficulties and focal points of activity:

- the pressure of environmentalist groups, mainly in Northern Europe;
- the accepted development of their field trials for transgenic products;
- marketing approval for their products;
- their marketing strategy, in terms of convincing farmers and their own international organization;
- intensive competition and the permanent threat of substitute technical systems for agriculture.

The other main group of actors is directly linked to food processing and retailing: as processors, ingredient producers and retailers. All of them deal with human food and, therefore, with concern about health risks. Their main problems are:

- pressure from consumer groups and their demand for information on the production process and products;
- marketing approval for their products;
- very competitive markets in which production costs and differentiation are key elements;
- creating a sophisticated production and logistics infrastructure.

Typology of Strategies in Risk Regulation and Risk Perception

Several kinds of strategy relating to risk regulation and risk perception can be distinguished among companies. Conclusions from research managed by the Rathenau Institute in the Netherlands (Tils, 1995) indicate that companies attempt to influence risk perception according to the following criteria:

- the importance of new biotechnology for the company;
- the characteristics of the competition;
- the acceptance sensitivity of the market;
- the development time for a product;
- the distance to the consumer;
- their position within the commercial chain;
- the product or brand dependency of the company;
- size and experience of the company in areas such as public affairs and public relations.

The gap of expertise and resources between major companies and small biotech companies in dealing with regulation is an important reason for understanding networking and alliance strategies being established by both categories of firm. However, other important factors should not be forgotten; these include the externalization and contractualization of basic research activity by major companies; the financial problems of small biotech companies; and the lack of time and resources of small biotech companies to take on direct commercialization (Assouline and Chataway, 1995).

The possible answer to heterogeneous (from one country to another) environmental pressures on the potential risk of GMOs' dissemination is to locate field trials in the most favourable areas: the most favourable countries are the Netherlands and France. National regulations, social context and significance of agriclimatic conditions are key factors influencing decisions about where to implement field trials.

Overall strategy, which is also influenced by a company's relations with other companies, retailers, government agencies and NGOs, can be characterized by the following broad types (Tils, 1995). Tils outlines three types of strategy:

Strategy I: Technology and Regulation as Competitive Barriers.
Technology Push: First Technology and Product Development, then Provide Information and Initiate Persuasion

R&D activities are managed by a development committee to achieve two priorities: controlling technology and targeting products with promising commercial prospects. Development committees are usually composed of marketing, industrial, R&D and legal affairs directors. Forecasts about social desirability of the products are made on the basis of companies' own scenarios.

Activities that are aimed at gaining public acceptance are only initiated when problems arise with the acceptance of a new biotechnology-related product, under societal pressure. These are mainly communication and marketing activities (such as videos and educational programmes).

Many French companies, due to the specific French context, could be classified within this group. Some US companies, for instance Monsanto, also tend to follow this strategy. Their no-risk position on GMO dissemination and their attempt to avoid food labelling for biotechnology-derived foods are expressions of the technology-push logic. In general, the further the company from the final consumer, the more its intervention hinges on the regulatory management of environmental risks.

Strategy II: Cost and Differentiation as Competitive Tools on the Final Consumer Market. An Attempt to Match Technology Push and Social Demand

R&D priorities are defined and implemented with some flexibility, according to the reaction of different social groups. In exchange for the acceptance of possible modifications, negotiations are carried out to reach a consensus. This means that the R&D decision-making process is quite open to substantial change and that information and debate are accepted at the early stages. Most of the important Dutch actors in agro-biotechnology are following this orientation. In Northern European countries, participation in public debate is considered by companies as a way to influence opinion and social groups, and also to make sure that they are developing and investing in products which respond to social needs. In the UK, the Technology Foresight exercise (Advisory Council on Science and Technology, 1994) insists that public perception needs to be taken into account by the industry, whatever the rationality or irrationality of this public perception. The closer the company is to the final consumer, the more it will be concerned by public perceptions about health risks. If we consider, for instance, the case of herbicide-resistant varieties, pressure from NGOs is certainly being taken into account more by crop processors and retailers than by bioproduct developers.

These industry managers see a need to be involved in public debate and to have relations with consumer groups. They are participating in negotiations to get a consensus on labelling, as is happening in Britain and the Netherlands. In the Netherlands, an agreement on labelling regulation has been developed between industry and consumer groups. Three kinds of product have been defined: products which must be labelled; products which do not need labelling; and points for further consultation. Products which need to be labelled are: transgenic animals; transgenic plants as genetically modified food crops containing either proteins which do not occur naturally in the relevant product or have been given changed consumption properties; tomatoes with an extended shelf life, pesticide-resistant maize; micro-organisms as products or ingredients which contain genetically modified micro-organisms, whether or not inactivated; dairy products with modified microcultures; bread yeast ingredients and additives (Informal Consultation Group on Biotechnology, 1995).

Although there appears to be a high level of consensus between NGOs and industry in this case, this may be more fragile than it first appears. In practice, there are problems with the types of labelling proposed and it is difficult to anticipate the kinds of interaction that could be developed between the two categories of industrial actors in cases of strong tension, such as the threat of a boycott campaign against biotechnology-derived food in an important market.

Strategy III: Wait and See Position

Some important companies prefer to have a low profile position, working on research and new products in their own country, or preferably in other countries such as France and the US for trials and the US for research, but waiting for other companies to do the job and create irreversibility in terms of approval, regulation and acceptance. Some German and Swiss companies could be included in such a category, due to the specific constraints posed by their national contexts, which have been very sceptical about biotechnology.

As more and more companies get nearer the marketing stage, the most favoured strategy is likely to become strategy II. As part of their marketing effort at least, companies wish to demonstrate that their products fulfil a social demand. Additionally, as we have argued earlier, companies are tending not to adopt high profile campaigns which promote the technological promise of biotechnology and oppose risk regulation. They are increasingly managing risk regulation and perception in a way which conforms more to an adaptive approach to coping with uncertainty. Companies which have adopted a 'wait and see' position will either decide they are too far behind to enter the race at all or will make significant efforts to catch up.

NEW CONCERNS AND THE FUTURE OF THE DEBATE

The Changing Nature of the Debate

If the terms of the debate about risk regulation have changed, they are certainly no less controversial and complex. A less technocratic approach to uncertainty and a less clear-cut position among industrialists towards risk regulation have made debate about harmonization, standardization, communication and the boundaries within which risk regulation should operate more complicated rather than less. The tenets upon which industry based its arguments about risk regulation have been called into question and regulators are also feeling new pressures. Regulators wish to construct regulatory codes that are efficient and effective. They are also keen that their activities are seen to be legitimate, and yet they are increasingly worried about the extent to which they will be 'blamed' from all sides if the balance is not right (Levidow et al., 1996).

At the same time, more companies are bringing products to market and products which are being internationally marketed are forcing consideration of new issues. Two examples demonstrate some of the problems facing companies and regulators:

Case A: Ciba Geigy's Bt-resistant transgenic corn[4]
One of the best examples of Europe's specific contextual problems and the contradictory nature of the situation is provided by the case of Ciba Geigy's Bt-resistant corn. This variety received final approval in the US in 1995 and has already been in full-scale production there. In 1996 it was submitted to the EU for marketing approval. According to French regulators, Ciba Geigy received the green light from the Commission du Genie Biomoleculaire in 1996. The European Commission expressed its agreement to approve the variety, but this process was blocked by the European Council of Environment Ministers during the summer of 1996 by 14 votes to 15. The Commission then asked three specialized scientific

committees to assess the risks for human and animal nutrition and the environment. Finally, in November 1996, the Commission, with reference to economic pressures, gave marketing approval, despite strong internal opposition. This, however, did not bring the debate to an end. France, which had been very active in pressuring the Commission to approve the marketing of the variety, itself prohibited internal production. It has, however, been cleared for human and animal consumption. In September, the variety was approved in Japan.

Case B: the Monsanto Roundup herbicide-resistant soybean[5]

Since the spring of 1996, Monsanto has been trying to market a new transgenic soybean variety called RRS (Roundup Ready Soybean), which is resistant to Roundup herbicide. Imports of this transgenic product have been allowed into Europe. The plan is to allow soybean imports from the US into Europe. This variety will be mixed with conventional soybeans. These imports are pressuring all food industry stakeholders to use GMOs in an undifferentiated way. EU regulations do not require any labelling. The first exports from the US to Europe have given rise to extreme opposition from NGOs which are arguing that all GMO products need to be labelled. Monsanto says that separating the GMO soybean in order to label it would be too expensive.

What both these cases show is the difficulty that Europe will have in enforcing its own regulatory codes. If Europe does not accept the transgenic and non-transgenic US corn, it would be considered by the US government to be in non-compliance with World Trade Organization agreements and the case will be fought on these grounds. In an official declaration to Greenpeace, the US Department of Agriculture explained that all agricultural trade to Europe could eventually contain GMOs. Objections to such exports could be considered an obstacle to free trade (Greenpeace, 1996).

NGOs opposing this are not so much arguing about the specificities of deliberate release risk regulation regimes. They are arguing that, on ethical grounds and because they consider all forms of testing and regulation to be severely limited, all GMO foods must be labelled.

CONCLUSION

Specific EU directives governing deliberate release at one time generated intense and acrimonious discussions between those who favoured and those who opposed horizontal and vertical forms of regulation. However, the EU directives are no longer the sole focal point of the debate; rather, discussions have forked off in a number of directions. A growing number of diverse regulatory, industry and NGO groups involved in the debate think that existing regulations, with modifications such as fast track procedures, can be worked with. Managers in many companies are concerned with how to manage regulations rather than with how to achieve deregulation.

Some companies, however, continue to push for regimes of risk regulation based on technocractic strategies for dealing with uncertainty. Some NGOs have responded to this by inverting the technocratic approach in order to argue that if quantifiable risk analysis cannot guarantee zero risk, there should be no release at all.

Questions concerned with where the boundaries of risk regulation should be placed, harmonization, and communication and information are all important parts of the current debate about risk regulation. These can be thought of as concerns about formulating adaptive strategies to cope with uncertainty and manage risk. In particular, issues regarding monitoring and learning continuously, prioritizing, collecting and disseminating analysis and information are likely to be central to future debates. The associated issue of labelling is becoming a key strategic issue for industry. This issue brings a new set of questions about how risk regulations and international trade agreements will impact on one another. Resistance to imports of unlabelled GMO products from the US is being challenged with reference to international trade regulations. Recent food scares in Europe have provoked new awareness about potential risks posed by new technologies. On the one hand, then, there is pressure from the free trade lobby to harmonize regulation on a global basis, but on the other hand there are are also renewed calls within Europe for the precautionary principle to inform risk regulation.

While this chapter has considered agro-food applications of biotechnology, the broader dynamics of the debate about management of uncertainty and risk regulation are equally important to medical and pharmaceutical applications of biotechnology. Although there are clearly differences, similar tensions between technocratic and adaptive approaches are also present in this area. Purely technocratic approaches are likely to be particularly ineffective in dealing with concerns about genetic engineering in the medical and pharmaceutical spheres.

NOTES

1. The study (Chataway, Assouline and Ruivenkamp 1996) was funded by the BIOTECH programme of the European Commission, DG XII.
2. Fieldwork in the Netherlands was carried out by Dr Guido Ruivenkamp from the University of Wageningen.
3. Tait distinguishes between process-based (usually associated with horizontal regulatory codes) and product-based (usually associated with vertical regulatory codes) in the following way: 'A process-based approach can be defined as one where (i) all products derived from the process of genetic manipulation, and designed to be released into the environment, are considered to have the potential to give rise to unique environmental hazards, not possessed by previous generations of products; and (ii) we need to devise new types of environmental oversight and regulation to ensure that any products giving rise to environmental hazards are excluded from further commercial development. A product-based approach is defined as one where: (i) it is assumed that GMOs do not present any unique environmental hazards arising from the process by which they were developed; and (ii) any environmental hazards that they do possess can be regulated effectively by the systems set up to deal with foods, drugs and pesticides' (Tait, 1990, p. 27).
4. The main source of information for this case study is Agro-Distribution (1996).
5. The main source of information for this case study is the same as for case study A.

REFERENCES

Acha, V. (1997), 'Policy development under uncertainty', in Part 4, TU870 *Capacities for Managing Development*, London: Sage Publications.

Advisory Council on Science and Technology (1994), *Technology Foresight. The Identification and Promotion of Emerging and Generic Technologies*, London: HMSO.

Agro-Distribution (1996), 'OGM: l'Europe entre deux chaises', Novembre, Paris.

Assouline, G. and J. Chataway (1995), *Global Industrial Competition and European Biotechnology Research and Innovation: Policy, Limits, Constraints and Priorities*, Energy and Research Series Working Paper W-17, Luxembourg: European Parliament.

Chataway, J. (1992), *The Making of Biotechnology: A Case Study of Radical Innovation*, PhD Thesis, Milton Keynes: Open University.

Chataway, J. and J. Tait (1993), 'Risk regulation and strategic decision making in biotechnology: the political economy of innovation', *Agriculture and Human Values*, **10**(2), 60–7.

Chataway, J., G. Assouline and G. Ruivenkamp (1996), *Risk Perception, Regulation and the Management of Agro-Biotechnologies*, Final Report for the Biotechnology Programme (BIOTECH) of the European Community, DG XII, Swavesey: Segal Quince Wickstead.

Commission of the European Communities (1993), *Growth, Competitiveness, Employment: The Challenges and Ways Forward into the 21st Century*, White Paper, COM (93) 700 final, Brussels: CEC.

Ernst & Young (1995), *European Biotechnology 95. Gathering Momentum*, London: Ernst & Young International.

Greenpeace (1996), *Press release on GMOs*, 6 November, Paris.

House of Lords Select Committee on Science and Technology (1993), *Regulation of the UK Biotechnology Industry and Global Competitiveness*, HL Papers 80-I and 80-II, London: HMSO.

Informal Consultation Group on Biotechnology (1995), *Market Introduction and Labelling of Foods Produced with the Aid of Modern Biotechnology (Genetic Modification)*, the Netherlands.

Kidd, G. and J. Dvorak (1994), 'A gutsy map of the future of agbiotech', *Bio/Technology*, **12**(11), 1064–5.

Kraus, M. (1994), *Regulation and Competitiveness of the European Biotechnology Industry*, Working Paper, Luxembourg: Directorate General for Research, European Parliament.

Levidow, L., S. Carr, R. von Schomberg and D. Wield (1996), 'Regulating agricultural biotechnology in Europe: harmonisation difficulties, opportunities, dilemmas', *Science and Public Policy*, **23**(3), 135–57.

SAGB (1990), *Community Policy for Biotechnology: Economic Benefits and European Competitiveness*, Brussels: CEFIC.

SAGB (1994), *Biotechnology Policy in the European Union: Prescriptions for Growth, Competitiveness and Employment*, Brussels: CEFIC.

Shohet, S. (1996), 'Biotechnology in Europe: contentions in the risk regulation debate', *Science and Public Policy*, **23**(2), 117–22.

Tait, J. (1990), *Biotechnology. Interactions between Technology, Environment and Society*, Technology Policy Group, Occasional Paper 20, Milton Keynes: Open University.

Tait, J. and L. Levidow (1992), 'Proactive and reactive approaches to regulation: the case of biotechnology', *Futures*, **24**(3), 219–31.

Tils, C. (1995), *Dutch Biotechnology Policy. A Practical Network Approach for Companies, Government and Societal Groups*, Den Haag: Rathenau Institute.

Zechendorf, B. (1994), 'What the public thinks about biotechnology', *Bio/Technology*, **12**(9), 870–75.

5. The creation of European dedicated biotechnology firms

Pier Paolo Saviotti, Pierre-Benoît Joly, Jacqueline Estades, Shyama Ramani and Marie-Angéle de Looze

As was pointed out in the Introduction and in Chapter 3, the biotechnology-based industries have an industrial structure characterized by the presence of three actors: large, diversified firms (LDFs), public research institutions (university or R&D laboratories) and dedicated biotechnology firms (DBFs). Among these the DBF is the newest actor. Small, high technology firms exist and play a very important role in other technologies (for example, IT, new materials), but DBFs are predominantly a phenomenon of the US. In the study on which this chapter is based (de Looze et al., 1996),[1] we tried to explain both the small number of DBFs in Europe and to study their capabilities with respect to those of the US. Since there is evidence that the role of European DBFs differs from that of their US counterparts, we use the term 'SMEs/DBFs' for European small and medium-sized biotechnology firms.

The presence of SMEs/DBFs is not the only novel feature of the prevailing industrial structure in biotechnology. The three actors do not act independently, but have many types of collaboration. Collaborations, ranging from joint R&D to joint production, are indeed the norm in biotechnology. In this industrial structure, SMEs/DBFs are not substitutes for LDFs, but often play complementary or interactive roles, being linked to LDFs and to public research organizations by contracts and alliances. For example, a new role which seems to have been acquired by SMEs/DBFs is that of intermediaries between LDFs and public research organizations, transferring knowledge between the two. This and other roles that SMEs/DBFs can play are dependent on their capacity to create and assimilate knowledge. Thus our study was concerned with the competences and knowledge bases of SMEs/DBFs and with the overall process of knowledge generation and accumulation in biotechnology.

Our main research objectives were to compare the pattern of formation of SMEs/DBFs in Europe and the US, and to study the relative capabilities of SMEs/DBFs in the two geographic areas. Among the factors which can influence firm creation and development we were particularly interested in the availability of capital, the role of strategic alliances, and the mechanisms of knowledge generation and accumulation.

Two main tools were used: a postal questionnaire and face-to-face interviews. The postal questionnaire was sent to French firms, face-to-face interviews were conducted with French and British firms, and Danish firms were both interviewed and sent a postal questionnaire. The detailed results obtained from this study are described in a report prepared for the European Commission (EC) (de Looze et al., 1996). An abbreviated form of our results is presented here, and is divided into sections about the postal questionnaire and the face-to-face interviews, respectively.

CREATION AND DEVELOPMENT OF SMEs/DBFs IN THE EUROPEAN UNION (EU)

The postal questionnaire was designed to gather information about several aspects of European SMEs/DBFs which would be comparable with data about US DBFs. Out of questionnaires sent to 383 firms, taken from the Annuaire ADEBIO, 79 responses were obtained, 18 were returned without an answer (the firm or the director did not exist) and 21 were not SMEs according to our definition.

The creation of the firms in our sample commenced in the early 1980s, with the rate of creation accelerating in the second half of the decade (see Figure 5.1).

The situation shown is similar to that in the US, with a lag. Clearly, according to our and other data (Dibner, 1995; Ernst &Young, 1995), the number of SMEs/DBFs in the EU continues to lag behind that in the US. However, the developments discussed in Chapter 2 might change this imbalance.

Main Features of the French Sample

The foundation of European and French firms began in the 1970s but developed mostly in the 1980s, lagging behind the US by about five years. The firms are similar regarding size, capital at foundation and turnover. French SMEs/DBFs are highly R&D intensive (20 per cent of their personnel work in R&D), though possibly less so than their US counterparts. The SMEs/DBFs in our sample are very intensive users and

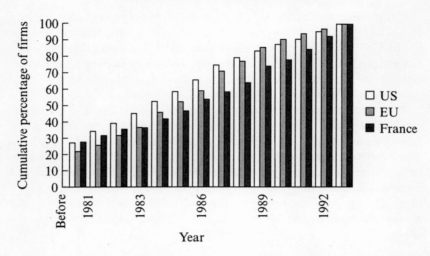

Sources: US – Dibner (1995); EU – Ernst & Young (1995); France – de Looze et al. (1996).

*Figure 5.1   Cumulative percentage of biotechnology SMEs/DBFs created in
            the US, EU and France*

creators of human resources, entering frequently into collaborations and
having a high rate of participation in national and EC research programmes. The SMEs/DBFs in the French sample tend to produce a
relatively high number of patents and publications for firms of their size:
43 per cent of the responding firms had at least one patent and 58 per
cent had at least one publication. Another important characteristic of the
firms in the French sample is the international nature of their markets:
83 per cent of the firms had a European market, 49 per cent a US
market, and 28 per cent an Asian market. In summary, the French
SMEs/DBFs in our sample are small, very R&D intensive and concentrated on R&D as a function, with a high propensity to produce patents
and papers, and a very international outlook.

Main Features of the Danish Sample

The Danish sample is much smaller than the French one, due both to the
small size of the country and to an industrial structure dominated by relatively large firms (for example, Novo Nordisk). Out of a sample of   11
firms, six replied to our questionnaire. Even within this limited sample, one
firm, founded relatively early (in 1960), fell outside the definition of SMEs
adopted in this study (≤500 employees), since it had 630 employees in 1994.

Given the small size of the sample, no systematic statistical analysis was possible, and we can do no more than provide some general comments. Danish SMEs/DBFs share a number of characteristics with those of the French sample. They are highly R&D intensive (on average 39 per cent of their personnel work in R&D) and have a high propensity to collaborate with universities and with other firms (see de Looze et al., 1996, Table 4). On the other hand, there are some differences which are worth pointing out. None of the firms benefited from any public support at the time of their foundation, and none participated in national or EC research programmes. Moreover, the distribution of firms by industrial sector seems to be peculiar: three firms out of six are primarily in the pharmaceutical sector and a fourth one, although concentrated on chemicals, is involved in DNA synthesis. Also, for four out of six firms, the most important markets are the US and Europe. In fact, the US is even more important for Danish than for French firms per cent (66 per cent of Danish firms had sales in the US compared to 49 per cent of French Firms). Thus, while confirming the high research intensity and propensity to collaborate generally found in other SMEs/DBFs, the Danish firms seem to have a very low dependence on public support or programmes, whether national or EC, to be more heavily concentrated in the pharmaceutical sector and, in view of the fact that Danish firms also have an Asian market, to be even more international in their outlook than their French counterparts.

TECHNOLOGICAL SPECIALIZATION OF SMEs/DBFs: COMPARISON BETWEEN FRANCE AND THE US

Statistical analysis of the French sample and other information shows that in comparison with the US there was a considerable lag in the rate of creation of biotechnology SMEs/DBFs in Europe and France for the period up to 1994.

Technological Diversity and Capabilities of the Firms

Recent developments in Germany (Jaeckel et al., 1994; Coombs and Alston, 1995) suggest that the gap between numbers of US and European DBFs is decreasing. However, the problem of relatively small numbers of European SMEs/DBFs could be compounded by their capabilities relative to those of their US counterparts. Thus we tried to develop methods that would allow us to assess the relative capabilities of biotechnology firms. We did this by asking a number of questions: first, is the knowledge base available to biotechnology firms homogeneous and undifferentiated or has it started to differentiate and to specialize? If there is an emerging pattern of specialization, what are its determinants? Are there any subsets of biotechnology which can be considered the frontier of knowledge and others that have become more evenly shared among biotechnology firms? In order to answer these questions we conducted a number of analyses on the data obtained from the questionnaires sent to French firms. First, we performed a factor analysis[2] of the technologies used by the SMEs/DBFs in the sample. Second, we applied a form of bibliometric analysis – 'Leximappe' – to the technologies used by the same sample of firms. Both these techniques identified the presence of groupings of inter-related technologies among the general set of technologies available to the firms. Factor analysis detects the presence of common components among the variables studied. The variables contained within the same component interact more strongly than those belonging to different components. Leximappe is a program[3] that allows us to construct a network of associated words to analyse its morphology. The association between two keywords is defined as the probability of having one of them when the other one is present. Using Leximappe we can characterize a scientific or technological theme by means of the average value of its internal links, or *density*, and by the total number of links with words which are not part of the same theme (external links), or *centrality*. Centrality thus depends both on the links between different themes and on those between themes and isolated words. Our factor analysis detected the following five groups of technologies: production processes, diagnostics, protein and cellular cultures, instrumentation, and genetic engineering (See Table 5.1). Such groupings have considerable plausibility: production processes (purification, filtration, fermentation, high pressure liquid chromatography) and instrumentation are general purpose techniques applicable to a wide range of problems which, in some cases, pre-date genetic engineering. Diagnostics is a relatively self-contained set of technologies, while genetic engineering represents the most novel component of modern biotechnology. The groups identified by Leximappe are similar and can be identified by the same categories, but their internal composition is slightly different (see Table 5.1). Such differences between the results of the two techniques are to be expected. Indeed their similarity contributes to the plausibility of our results.

In spite of the great differences in the nature of the data used, our results have something in common with those obtained by McCain (1995). Our three groups, TG1 = production processes, TG3 = proteins and cellular cultures and TG5 = genetic engineering, have the same two foci – fermentation and genetics/cell culture – found in the structure of publications and patents in her study. The two additional groups of diagnostics and instrumentation are probably due to the different nature of

Table 5.1 Technological groups (TGs) resulting from factor analysis and Leximappe

	Classification based on factor analysis	Classification based on Leximappe	Technological orientation
TG1	Purification Fermentation Filtration	HPLC Purification Fermentation Filtration Others	Production processes
TG2	Kits Immunological products Cellular fusion Hybridoma Antibodies	Antibodies Immunological products Cellular fusion Hybridoma Biochemical reagents	Diagnostic
TG3	Biochemical reagents Peptides Protein Synthesis Protein sequencing Cellular cultures Electrophoresis Microscopy Spectroscopy	Kits Imaging Peptides	Proteins Cellular cultures
TG4	Hardware/software Robotics Monitoring Imaging	Robotics Microscopy Spectroscopy Electrophoresis Cellular cultures	Instrumentation
TG5	DNA probes DNA synthesis DNA sequencing Gene amplification	DNA probes DNA sequencing DNA synthesis Gene amplification Hardware/software	Genetic engineering

our data. Bearing in mind the limitations previously described in our data, we can conclude that although processes of specialization in biotechnology may not be very advanced, a structure is emerging. Such structure can be interpreted in terms of two main foci: those of production processes and of genetic engineering-based techniques. Instrumentation and diagnostics are two additional groupings, defined by general research and production tools in the first case, and by a specific application in the second.

Technological Specialization and Applications

In addition to detecting the emergence of various groupings, Leximappe allowed us to compare the behaviour of US and French SMEs/DBFs regarding these emerging patterns of specialization. We can plot the technologies of our sample in a space defined by the two axes of centrality and density. We reproduce here only the data for firms which are predominantly involved in R&D for France (Figure 5.2) and the US (Figure 5.3).[4] The analysis of the results is difficult because the technologies used are not exactly the same in the two countries. However, some technologies, such as cell culture, hybridoma, protein engineering and genetic engineering, are common to both countries. Indeed genetic engineering is one of the central technologies for this type of firm, and is a technology strongly related to all the others. On the other hand, only the US has firms specializing in new areas of gene therapy, DNA antisense and gene transfer. These emerging areas give weak signals, but these signals have been detected for several years. Thus while some of the knowledge base is common to French and US SMEs/DBFs, US firms seem to be making advances in some areas which are on the technological frontier.

After performing this analysis on the extent of technological specialization/differentiation in our sample of firms, we investigated possible relationships between the extent of specialization and some other aspects of a firm. We found no relationship between technological specialization/differentiation and the main function performed by the firm (research, development, services). Instead we found a correlation between groups of technologies and fields of application. For example, the technological group 'production processes' is related to the application 'cell culture', 'bioseparation', 'nutrition', and 'fermentation' (see Table 5.2). These results imply that the limited extent of technological specialization existing in our sample of firms is related to their fields of application.

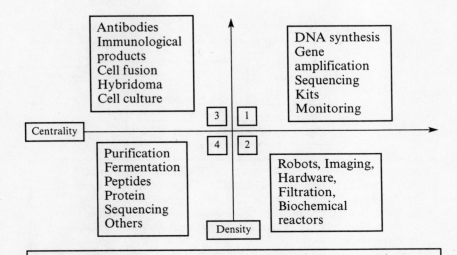

For 47 firms which replied that they carry out R&D, the technologies DNA synthesis, gene amplification, sequencing kits and monitoring are strongly linked among themselves and even more strongly linked to the technologies found in the other quadrants.
The technologies of quadrant 2, without being strongly linked among themselves, are strongly linked to the technologies of the other quadrants.
The technologies of quadrant 3, strongly linked together, are weakly linked to other applications.
Note: the firms that provide mainly R&D replied that they also carry out development (37 cases) and services (29 cases) work.

Figure 5.2 Results of Leximappe analysis for French firms mainly involved in R&D

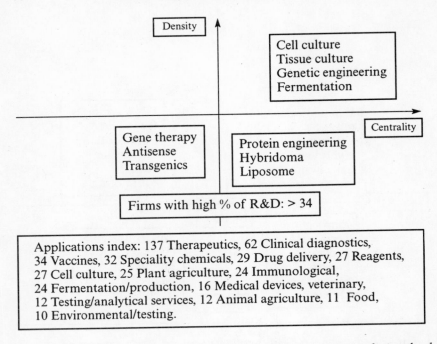

Figure 5.3   Results of Leximappe analysis for US firms mainly involved in R&D

TECHNOLOGICAL INNOVATION STRATEGIES OF SMEs/DBFs IN FRANCE AND BRITAIN

This section analyses interviews conducted with 13 French firms and ten British firms. The interviews were very extensive (for questionnaire see appendix of de Looze et al., 1996) and were conducted with the chief executive officers of the firms who, in many instances, were also the founders. All the firms interviewed had been established recently: two were created before 1980, ten were created between 1980 and 1985, eight were created between 1985 and 1990, and four were created after 1990. The technological competences of all 23 firms corresponded to what could be termed 'modern biotechnology'. In both countries a majority of the firms were founded by academic researchers (60 per cent in France and 57 per cent in Britain). While the small sample of firms may not adequately represent the population, these in-depth interviews threw light on some facts and trends which could not be found from secondary data. The 'interview method' is particularly relevant for testing theories about

Table 5.2 Relationship between technological groups and applications

Technological groups	TG1 Production	TG2 Diagnostics	TG3 Proteins	TG4 Instrumentation	TG5 DNA
Applications					
DIAGNOSTICS		+		+	+
RESEARCH		+	+	+	+
DRUGS					
CELL CULTURE	+		+		+
REAGENTS		+	+		+
PRODUCTS FOR IMMUNOLOGY		+	+		
WASTES/ ENVIRONMENT		–			
VACCINES			+		+
BIOSEPARATIONS	+			+	
FINE CHEMICALS					
TEST/ANALYSIS EXPERTISE		+	+		
NUTRITION	+				
FERMENTATION/ PRODUCTION	+				
VEGETABLE AGRICULTURE			+	+	
VETERINARY APPLICATIONS					+
GENE THERAPY		+	+		+
ANIMAL AGRICULTURE				+	
EQUIPMENT					+
BIOSENSORS				+	+
MEDICAL EQUIPMENT					
THERAPY			+		

+ 5%
+ 10%
– 10%

Note: The symbols in the cells of the table indicate positive or negative relationships significant to 10 or 5 degrees of confidence.

the evolution of firm competence, since information available through databases or postal questionnaires rarely reveals information of an evolutionary nature and, more importantly, rarely indicates the reasons why evolution occurred as it did. The objectives of the interviews were, first, to examine whether there were any significant differences in the evolutionary patterns of firm competences in the SMEs active in the biotechnology sectors in France and the UK and, second, to ascertain the reasons for any such differences.

Competences, Network and Technological Innovation Strategy: The Conceptual Framework for the Interviews

The concepts of competence, of networks and of technological innovation strategy played a very important role in constructing and interpreting these interviews. Competences have recently become an important concept in the interpretation of firm behaviour and performance. Edith Penrose (1959) provided a precursor to the competence approach when she described the firm as a 'bundle of capabilities'. Subsequently Teece (1986) studied the combination of what he called 'complementary assets' and Prahalad and Hamel (1990) defined the core competence of the corporation. These are just three examples of what has now become a general perspective for the interpretation of firm behaviour and performance. There is no standard definition of competences, but they can be considered as ways of transforming and combining elements of knowledge in order to achieve a firm's objectives. The elements of knowledge to be combined are not necessarily only scientific or technological, although these may contribute to the core competence of the corporation, as is often the case in biotechnology SMEs/DBFs. Competences can be classified as scientific, technological, marketing, legal and so on, and can be even further disaggregated (for example, microbiology, genetic engineering, recombinant DNA and so on).

The network approach has been developed by several authors (for example, Burt, 1980; Powell, 1990; Callon, 1991) and is becoming accepted increasingly as a mode of analysis. In spite of growing diffusion there is no general network theory. The authors who take a network perspective have very little in common except their interest in interactions between actors. This chapter has been inspired mostly by the work on socio-technical networks by Callon (1991). A socio-technical network is defined as a set of coordinated relations by heterogeneous actors: public laboratories, research centres, firms, financial organizations, consumers and public bodies, which participate collectively in the conception, elaboration, production and distribution or diffusion of the proceeds of production, the goods or the services which give rise to a market transaction (Callon 1991, p.196). Mustar (1995) conducted an empirical analysis of 100 firms created in France between 1983 and 1987 in selected high tech sectors to show that the viability of these firms depended on their insertion in a network connecting and drawing together different actors with different competences in different sectors.

Technology and innovation strategy is a subset of overall firm strategy. Freeman (1982) has classified innovation strategies as aggressive, defensive, imitative, dependent and traditional or opportunistic. An aggressive innovator would try to be first in introducing an innovation, a defensive innovator would try to be ready to follow as soon as possible, while imitative, dependent and traditional innovators would rely on adopting pre-existing innovations of growing maturity. In the case of biotechnology we expect innovators to be predominantly aggressive or defensive, given the relative novelty and the high science intensity of this technology. Of course we cannot rule out more imitative strategies, but we expect these to be far less common. In addition we can classify firms' technology strategies as widening or deepening, according to whether they tend to acquire new technologies or to improve their understanding and the performance of the technologies which they are already using. Of course the former strategy would lead to product differentiation while the latter would lead to a growing degree of specialization.

The three concepts of competences, networks and innovation/technology strategy are not independent. Competences are acquired by a firm both internally and by participating in networks. The choice of a particular innovation/technology strategy determines both the competences acquired and the types of network in which the firm can participate.

Network Structure and Technology Strategy of French and British SMEs/DBFs

The results of our interviews not only identified the networks formed by our sample firms, but also allowed us to classify them according to the main actors other than the firms studied. On the basis of a number of indicators derived from our interviews (see de Looze et al., 1996, Tables 9–11) we found six types of network, or networks with six different kinds of agent, which play a crucial role in the evolution of a firm's competence. They are: scientific networks, political networks, professional networks, financial networks, networks with large firms and networks with other SMEs (See Figure 5.4).

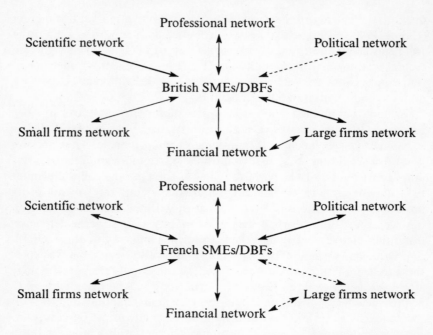

Figure 5.4 The network structure of French and British SMEs/DBFs

The analysis of the network structure of French and British firms gives the following results:

1. Scientific networks are crucial to the creation and evolution of firms in both France and Britain. In both countries, the scientific network fulfils five roles for the firm:
    (a) a reservoir for augmenting the knowledge base of the firm resulting from the proximity of the firm to the research laboratory (eight out of ten British firms and 12 out of 13 French firms);
    (b) a reservoir for recruiting personnel for R&D activities (scientists and engineers) (for three out of ten British firms and 12 out of 13 French firms);
    (c) a reservoir of complementary competences and resources for firms which share the local, instrumentation and established infrastructure (for four out of ten British firms and four out of 13 French firms);
    (d) a client for firms' products or services (for three out of ten British firms and nine out of 13 French firms);
    (e) a partner for developing new products or processes through research contracts or through supporting doctoral students (for nine out of ten British firms and 12 out of 13 French firms).

2. Large firms have only weak involvement in capital investments in French SMEs/DBFs, but they invest capital in British SMEs/DBFs. This is clear when we note that large firms had a capital stake in six out of ten SMEs/DBFs in Britain, but only in three out of 13 in France.
3. In both countries SMEs/DBFs have weak involvement in investments in other small biotechnology firms. The tally was zero firms in Britain and one out of 13 for France.
4. In France, networks with firms for the commercialization of innovations is not strong; this is not so for Britain. Seven out of ten British firms had a strategic alliance or a joint venture with a large firm to develop an innovation. Only three of the ten British firms had a strategic alliance or joint venture with another SME/DBF to develop an innovation.
5. In France, political networks constitute a far more important resource than in Britain. Only two out of ten British firms participated in EC programmes, while six out of 13 French firms did so. It is also clear that French firms were actively engaged in political networks, either as participants in expert committees or in national programmes (seven out of 13). It is to be noted that the firms in the two categories were not the same. The British firms were involved in political networks mainly through being recipients of national awards (five out of ten cases), but rarely as participants in any decision-making body (three out of ten cases).

The technology strategy of the firms in our sample was generally aggressive. The widely held stereotype of the non-imitating, technology-receiving SME does not fit biotechnology. In both the British and the French sample, the majority of firms adopted a technology-deepening strategy (seven out of ten UK firms and ten out of 13 French firms), with very few firms adopting a technology-widening strategy (one British firm and three out of 13 French firms). The majority of the firms that adopted a technology-widening strategy said that financial constraints were the main bottleneck to diversification of their competences. Survival for the innovative SME depends on technological leadership and for this they have to pursue a technology-deepening strategy, but they do not have enough funds to investigate new projects outside their existing competences. The only company that diversified its competences was forced to do so because of the limited market for its earlier product. It diversified its competences in order to be commercially viable.

Academic networks are very important in both countries. Fifty-seven per cent of the French firms and 60 per cent of the British firms emerged from the academic sector, indicating the academic sector as an important source for the emergence of firms. However, academic networks remained relatively more important to the later phases of development of French than of British firms. For eight out of ten British firms, the academic network was the crucial external linkage which acted as a resource for acquiring knowledge, but their technology strategy was determined by the needs of the market within which they functioned. Seven of the ten British firms were using strategic alliances, research collaborations or product co-development as a valuable source of funds. In turn, the needs of the large firm partners influenced the evolution of the competence of the SMEs/DBFs and the orientation of their knowledge base, even when there were no knowledge transfers.

It has been noted that venture capital played a role in the creation of 46 per cent of the French firms and 20 per cent of the British firms in our sample. Financial networks were crucial in determining the evolution of the competence of six of the 13 French firms; this was true in only one of the British firms. Thus venture capitalists play a crucial role in the emergence and evolution of SMEs/DBFs. However, there is an inherent tension between the creators of firms and venture capitalists because the activities which support the aims of the two types of actor are often in conflict with each other. For instance, the normal objective of venture capital firms is to realize their investments in new firms after three years, on average. They focus on finding a buyer for the firm when they wish to recover their capital. On the other hand, the founders of the firms do not wish to lose control of their firms or relinquish their power to take initiatives or make decisions.

The desire to 'stay French'[5] is very strong and was expressed by many of the French firms (six out of 13). It was based on two preoccupations: concerns about ownership and a desire to retain control of strategic decision making about management and technological orientation. In order to achieve this, the founders build financial networks with family members, friends and managers of firms known personally to the founder. From this perspective, venture capital firms are often viewed as lenders of last resort. In addition, a desire to protect the French base as the place where strategic decisions are made, reinforces the intention to 'stay French' when venture capitalists suggest bringing in foreign investors. Similarly, a buy-out of a French SME by an American company, often at the initiative of a venture capital firm, is regarded as an outflow of national research results. However, this does not imply that French firms do not enter into collaborative agreements with foreign companies; such agreements are simply limited to commercial ones for the distribution of products.

On the other hand, seven of the ten British firms in our sample had strategic alliances or collaborations with non-British firms or research institutes to develop innovations. Even for those which were partly or totally held by foreign companies, ownership issues were not a problem. Strangely enough, one hears here echoes of the gospel preached by the French venture capitalists, in that what the British firms see as important is the emergence of firms in Britain and not of their being British. However, they do not explain their attitude or indicate whether such an attitude would be beneficial or detrimental in the long run.

The British firms seem to have a network structure in which the use made of each partner in the network seems to be more specific than for the French firms. Research institutes are an essential backward linkage, providing a source of knowledge, while large firms form the forward linkage, being direct or indirect clients whose needs determine the technology strategy of the SME. In France, the desire to centralize decision making for technology strategy within the firm is translated into actions whereby networks with large firms, public laboratories or government bodies are used as resources to support the evolution of the SME, in the manner determined by its managers. Partners in the network do not determine the technology strategy of the SME, and the relationship with partners is more *ad hoc* and less specific than for British SMEs/DBFs.

Network Participation and Role of the SMEs/DBFs in the Production of Innovations

In biotechnology, the role of SMEs/DBFs depends on the degree of vertical integration of the firm and the size of its market. For instance, if an SME restricts itself to conducting research, it can survive through: (1) selling the product of its research outright, or through the sale of licences or patents; (2) conducting contract research for other firms; and (3) co-developing products with another firm. If an SME integrates into production, its activities can include: (4) producing for other firms through contracts; (5) co-producing products with another firm; and (6) producing own products for final consumption.

Under (1) and (2) the SME's role is to act as a 'scientific gatekeeper', translating scientific knowledge into usable technology for other firms. It acts as a source of 'complementary competence' to large firms, investigating the potential of science for commercialization. Under (4) it is simply a supplier.

Under (3) and (5) the SME enters into 'strategic alliances' with large firms to create innovations. This includes cooperation only at the R&D and production stage and not at the marketing stage. A strategic alliance is different from a market transaction or contract in that it involves joint control and joint decision making over particular resources for an agreed period of time.

Under (6) the SME has no direct relationship with large firms but may be of strategic interest to the large firms depending on the value of the innovation that the SME has created. For instance, if the SME creates a radical innovation or is a 'radical innovator', it enjoys a temporary monopoly of a potentially substantial market. The SME may or may not become a major rival to large firms, depending on the impact of the innovation on the present or future market shares of the large firms. On the other hand, if the SME has created an incremental innovation it might enjoy a local or even a global market, but the present and future size of the market is such as to constitute only a niche *vis-à-vis* the existing market share of the large firms. In this case, even if the SME operates in the same sector as the large firms it is not of strategic interest to the large firms.

Thus we can delineate the following relationships between the 'role of the SME' and the 'relationship between SMEs/DBFs and large firms'. Four roles have been identified for SMEs/DBFs in biotechnology. Furthermore, these four roles can give rise to a number of combinations and hybrids. In our interviews we found that the role played by an SME/DBF can have an important influence on the types of network it forms (see Table 5.3).

The objective of this exercise was to point out differences in the strategy and development patterns of SMEs/DBFs in France and Britain rather than to make any normative judgements on which pattern is better in the short or long run. Though the small size of the sample involved in interviews suggests that our results should be treated with caution, our results suggest that the evolution of the competence of SMEs/DBFs develops from their major resource, namely their network structure.

CONCLUSION

The point of departure of our study was the relative weakness of European SMEs/DBFs. Until recently such weakness could be measured by the considerably lower number of SMEs/DBFs in the European Union as compared with those of the US. Recent developments, especially in Germany, might lead to bridging of the numerical gap, but we have to bear in mind that estimates of the number of DBFs are highly dependent on the definition of biotechnology used. Without accepting this evidence as definitive, and bearing in mind the finding by Bullock and Dibner (1995) that the population of US DBFs stabilized in the second half of the 1980s, it seems that the numerical gap between US and European SMEs/DBFs is narrowing. However, this by no means implies that the technological capability gap is disappearing. A number of important differences still exist between

Table 5.3 Role of SMEs in the production of innovation and relationships with large firms

Activity of the SME	Type of role	French SMEs	British SMEs	Relationship with large firms
Just carrying out and selling research output	Scientific gatekeeper	38.5%	50%	Supplier of technical knowledge with commercial potential
Developing or producing product with other firms	Co-developer or co-producer	23%	30%	Possible strategic alliances with large firms
Producing own product with limited market share or size	Niche holder	30.75%	20%	Of no strategic interest to the large firms
Producing own product and either creating a new market or changing existing market shares of large firms	Radical innovator	7.5%	0%	Of possible strategic interest to the large firms

US and European SMEs/DBFs and between the environments in which they operate. For example, in spite of recent changes, the availability of venture capital is still more limited in Europe than in the US. Interestingly, European LDFs seem to purchase US and not European DBFs. On the other hand, European SMEs/DBFs are often purchased by US firms, although not necessarily by LDFs. These weaknesses and asymmetries point towards a vicious circle, in which low scientific and technological capabilities coupled with a scarcity of venture capital and with the absence of escape routes, can lead to SMEs/DBFs with weak development potential. Such SMEs/DBFs will not be attractive options for European LDFs looking to purchase firms as close as possible to the technological frontier. The general reasons why US firms buy European SMEs/DBFs, and the nature of the purchasing firms, is not yet clear.

It therefore seemed important to study the factors determining the stability of the industrial structure discussed in this study, and the relative capabilities of European and US SMEs/DBFs. The analysis of the technological competences of SMEs/DBFs is very important in both these problems. It is this analysis which we have developed using different tools and approaches. We performed a statistical analysis of data obtained from a postal questionnaire sent to a sample of French firms and of data contained in Dibner's database for US firms. We also studied the types of network formed by French and British firms and the role played by these networks in the development of firms. A version of the postal questionnaire was used in a study of Danish firms. However, due to the non-comparability of data (for example, between our French sample and Dibner's database) or to small sample sizes (particularly for UK and Danish firms), we could not apply all approaches to the complete set of French, UK, Danish and US firms. Nevertheless this study has produced two results:

1. First, we have developed a set of methodologies which seem to be well suited to the analysis of firms' capabilities and competences. Although such methodologies are not yet perfect and need to be improved, they represent an advance with respect to existing methods.
2. Second, we have been able to make some comparative analysis of French, UK, Danish and US SMEs/DBFs, although mostly on a bilateral basis and for specific aspects.

An important part of our analysis related to the knowledge base of SMEs/DBFs. It seems that, although patterns of technological specialization are not yet very pronounced, a structure is emerging. By means of indicators based on the diffusion and co-occurrence of technologies on the one hand, and on Leximappe on the other, we separated the technologies that are general purpose and widely used by all firms from those which determine the specialization and the competitive advantage of firms. We are not yet sure about the general significance of these results, but we think they are worth testing and exploring.

The results of the face-to-face interviews with a sample of French and UK firms identified six different types of network in which SMEs/DBFs participate. Analysis of the network structure of these SMEs/DBFs revealed two roles played by the different actors to which they are linked. First, they are a resource and, second, some actors in the network are influential in determining the short-term functioning and the long-term evolution of firms' technological competence.

We found that SMEs/DBFs can play several roles which are related to the types of relationship they have with LDFs. For example, a scientific gatekeeper is likely to be predominantly involved in supplying technical knowledge with commercial potential to an LDF, while a co-developer or co-producer can be involved in alliances with large firms. In the sample of firms examined, we found that the most frequent roles of SME/DBFs are as scientific gatekeeper and the complementary relationship as a supplier of technical knowledge. Creation of innovations through strategic alliances between SMEs/DBFs and LDFs is the exception rather than the rule. Obviously it is important to compare these trends and forms of behaviour with what happens in the US.

If we now return to our initial question, we found there was a numerical gap between US and European SMEs/DBFs during the 1980s and early 1990s. Although this numerical gap may be narrowing, an important capability gap is still perceived to exist, as demonstrated by the asymmetric investment patterns of European LDFs in the US and Europe. In spite of data limitations our approaches allowed us to identify some indications of a persisting capability gap between French and US SMEs/DBFs. Moreover, studies of French, British and Danish firms point towards both similarities and differences between European SMEs/DBFs.

We conclude by pointing out that the approaches used in this study could not only be improved, but interesting extensions of them could be developed in a number of ways. First, scope for the statistically based approach would be enhanced by greater data availability and comparability. Second, the relationship between firm capability and performance could be studied. Third, a comparison of different biotechnology-based industrial sectors could be undertaken.

NOTES

1. This study was financed by the BIOTECH programme of the European Commission, DG XII.
2. Factor analysis has been performed by Nadine Mandran, statistician at NRA, Grenoble.
3. This programme was developed by CSI, Ecole des Mines, Paris and CNRS.
4. The data for firms used in this analysis are taken from Dibner (1995).
5. Expressed in interviews.

REFERENCES

Bullock, W.O. and M.D. Dibner (1995), 'The state of the US biotechnology industry', *TIBTECH*, **13**, 463–7.
Burt, R.S. (1980), 'Models of network structure', *Annual Review of Sociology*, **6**, 79–141.
Callon, M. (1991), 'Réseaux technico-économiques et irréversibilités', in R. Boyer (ed.), *Les Figures de l'Irréversibilité en Economie*, Paris: Editions de l'Ecole des Hautes Etudes en Sciences Sociales, pp. 195–230.
Coombs, J. and Y.R. Alston (eds) (1995), *International Biotechnology Directory*, London: Macmillan Reference.
De Looze, M.A., J. Estades, P.B. Joly, S. Ramani, P.P. Saviotti, J. Senker and J.L. Pedersen (1996), *The Role of SMEs/DBFs in Technology Creation and Diffusion: Implications for European Competitiveness in Biotechnology*. A report for the European Commission, CT-942032, Grenoble: INRA-SERD.
Dibner, M.D. (1995), *Biotechnology Guide USA*, 3rd Edition, Research Triangle Park, NC: Institute for Biotechnology Information.
Ernst & Young (1995), *European Biotech 95. Gathering Momentum*, London: Ernst & Young International.
Freeman, C. (1982), *The Economics of Industrial Innovation*, London: Pinter Publishers.
Jaeckel, G., B. Husing, E. Strauss and T. Reiss (1994), *Analyse der Baden-Württembergischen F&E-Strukturen und -Potentiale in der Biotechnologie*. Studie im Auftrag der Akademie für Technikfolgenabschätzung in Baden-Württemberg, Karlsruhe: ISI.
McCain, K.W. (1995), 'The structure of biotechnology R&D', *Scientometrics*, **32** (2), 153–75.
Mustar, P. (1995), *Science et Innovation. Annuaire Raisonné de la Création D'entreprises par les Chercheurs*, Paris: Economica.
Penrose, E. (1959), *The Theory of the Growth of the Firm*, Oxford: Blackwell.
Powell, W. (1990), 'Neither market nor hierarchy: networks forms of organization', in B.N. Straw and L.L. Cummings (eds), *Research in Organizational Behavior*, **12**, pp 295–336.
Prahalad, C.K. and G. Hamel (1990), 'The core competence of the corporation', *Harvard Business Review*, May–June, 79–91.
Teece, D. (1986), 'Profiting from technological innovation', *Research Policy*, **15** (6), 285–305.

6. The evolution of European biotechnology and its future competitiveness

Rohini Acharya, Anthony Arundel
and **Luigi Orsenigo**

INTRODUCTION

The development of biotechnology in Europe is often compared and contrasted with the experience of technological leaders such as the US. The successful commercialization of biotechnology in the US is usually associated with the formation of the dedicated biotechnology firm (DBF) in the 1980s, which played the role of a 'system integrator', linking research from universities to market opportunities. The DBF was until recently non-existent in Europe, prompting increased interest in the role played by the DBF in the US and whether the state of European biotechnology would have been different today had the European DBF developed in the 1980s. While not seeking specifically to answer this question, the study on which this chapter is based, examines the role of the DBF and the part it has played in the different networks that have emerged in Europe and the US.

This chapter presents the basic theoretical framework of this study and summarizes some of its more significant conclusions. For further details on the research results, the reader is referred to the original project report.

Two stylized interpretations can be made with respect to the role of the DBF: first, DBFs can be analysed in terms of the 'industry life-cycle model'. Indeed a cursory analysis might suggest that the emergence and subsequent growth of the biotechnology industry is an example of the 'Schumpeter Mark I' model of technological change, with the early period of evolution characterized by a high rate of firm entry on the basis of product innovation (Klepper, 1992; Malerba and Orsenigo, 1996). As the industry evolves over time, increasing returns from economies of scale in R&D and production and cumulative innovation give early innovators an absolute advantage over incumbents, which face severe difficulties in adapting to the new technologies. The result is the displacement of incumbents, which are unable to adapt to the changes demanded by the new technology, by new entrants which become the new industrial and technological leaders in the sector. As the industry matures, there is a tendency towards increased concentration with entry and exit declining, and the number of firms in the industry becomes stable with innovators continuing to dominate and to grow rapidly (Klepper, 1992; Malerba and Orsenigo, 1996). The presence of a large number of small, innovative biotechnology companies, especially in the US and later in Europe, could be used as an example of this model of technological change.

A detailed analysis of the evolution of biotechnology in Europe and the US shows that the case of biotechnology presents several features that make it quite distinct from this traditional model. First, despite overwhelming evidence that incumbent companies were slower than new entrants to adopt and adapt the new technologies, rather than being swept away by the biotechnology entrants, a number of incumbents are today at the forefront of technological change and among the industrial leaders. Second, the relationship between the incumbent companies and the small entrants has been built not only on competition but also on cooperation and complex interactions between firms at various stages of research and product development.

We therefore move to a second stylized interpretation which rests on the premise that biotechnology depends upon a strong scientific base and its complex and interdisciplinary nature tends to make technological innovation the outcome of interacting agents (Orsenigo, 1989; Pisano, 1991; Sharp, 1995). The role of networks and differentiated agents within those networks becomes the locus of innovation, rather than the individual firm and competition between individual firms, as before. Collaboration between established corporations, DBFs and universities is a distinctive feature of the biotechnology industry. Moreover, the 'publicness' of science, which is an important component of the knowledge base, makes the development of new patterns for the division of labour among different agents more likely.

While there is a growing consensus that interaction between different agents involved in the commercialization of biotechnology is required for innovation, there is less clarity on the division of labour within each collaboration. A first interpretation stresses the role played by scientific knowledge in biotechnology (Arora and Gambardella, 1990; Gambardella, 1995). The fact that science is abstract and codified allows the innovation process, and therefore the role of individual agents, to be divided along a linear process going from science to application, production and marketing. From this point of view, collaboration between these agents is likely to be permanent. A second interpretation argues that the innovation process involves the integration of a range of activities which cannot be separated easily (Henderson, 1994), causing difficulties in integrating different pieces of knowledge along the cycle of innovation and commercial production. The DBFs would therefore seek to overcome these problems by trying to become vertically integrated (Pisano, 1991). Thus collaboration will tend to be transitory, especially in the early stages of the development of the industry. In the long run, collaboration will either disappear or the collaborative network will tend to become more centralized with a small number of firms clustering around large companies with stable interactions with other such constellations. Collaboration may also continue along a horizontal trajectory with collaboration between companies which are vertically integrated, but in different niches.

While these are two extreme views, they provide a framework for examining the role played by collaboration in developing the respective roles of DBFs, Multinational companies (MNCs) and public research in R&D networks. The study uses this framework to guide an examination of the evolution of the industrial structure of commercial biotechnology in Europe and the role played by DBFs. In Europe, technological innovation in biotechnology has lagged behind the US and the European biotechnology sector contains very few DBFs. An important question, therefore, is whether DBFs are an essential requirement for progress in this sector, for example as a result of the need for a system integrator, or if the function of the DBF in the US can be replaced by the large companies that have played a more dominant role in Europe.

The analysis uses a number of different approaches to study particular relationships between and within networks in greater detail. These include an analysis of patent data from the European Patent Office (EPO), data on collaborative agreements between companies exchanging technological knowledge and, finally, in-depth company and institutional interviews in three European countries; that is, Italy, the Netherlands and the United Kingdom. In each, we focus on the role of the DBF in Europe and its institutional and research environments.

PATENT ANALYSIS

The fundamental role of technological innovation and the development of a dense network of collaborative relationships between a variety of different actors have been distinctive features of the evolution of biotechnology. The birth of the industry was made possible by the development of new, major technological opportunities and it continues to be driven by technological innovation. Although other competences such as marketing are increasingly becoming a fundamental factor in determining success and failure, the ability to generate fast technological progress has always been the key element that determines the competitiveness of firms and is likely to remain so in the future.

The DBFs that were formed in the US as spin-offs from university research in order to exploit the new technological opportunities commercially first propelled biotechnology into the front pages. Large, established corporations that dominated the market at the time were much slower to react, and continue in large part to rely on various forms of collaborative links with DBFs in order to enter the emerging industry. In Europe and Japan, while the large companies reacted in the same way as in the US, small, DBF-type companies were conspicuously absent, the result being that the biotechnology industry was much slower to emerge. In fact, much of the role performed by the DBF in the US was taken over by the public research network in Japan and Europe (Orsenigo, 1989).

In order to study the adequacy of the current structure in Europe to enable and sustain future competitiveness in this industry, one must begin with an analysis of these two phenomena, and particularly with an assessment of the role of the DBFs as carriers and enablers of innovation and industrial transformation. Collaboration between firms could be interpreted either as a permanent or transitory phenomenon which is bound to decline in importance as the industry matures and industrial relationships change.

The analysis of the patent data looks at how the structure of innovative activities and collaboration has evolved over time. The analysis was based on the EPO/Cespri dataset, based on patent applications made at the EPO over the period 1978–93. The obvious drawback in using data on patent applications is that not all applications are granted a patent. However, the use of patent applications over time gives some indication of innovative activities in Europe. In this particular case, the EPO patent data for the earliest years may underestimate the actual level of innovative activities because the EPO had only just been founded and firms may have taken time to file their patents with this new institution. Similarly, given the time lag of around two years before a patent application is granted or denied, these data are likely to reflect innovative activities only up to 1990–91. In order to evaluate the evolution of innovative activities over time, the database was divided into two sub-periods: 1978–86 and 1987–93. In addition, a relatively strict definition – the technological class C12N of the International Patent Classification – was used as the main indicator of innovative activities in biotechnology.[2]

A simple count of the number of patent applications in each time period shows that American firms accounted for 43.1 per cent of patent applications in the first time period, followed by Japanese firms at 19.6 per cent and German firms at 10.6 per cent. The share of the seven most active European countries combined, however, is 30.9 per cent. During the second time period the relative share of American patents declined slightly to 41.7 per cent, while the share of European patents increased in each of the seven countries, with the combined share increasing to 40.2 per cent.

Each firm with at least one biotechnology patent is counted as a biotechnology innovator. The relative number of innovators again is largest in the US and twice that of Japan. In Europe, Germany has the largest number of innovators, with France and the UK following at a distance. Small countries such as Switzerland, the Netherlands and Denmark, however, show a relatively large number of innovators compared with their absolute sizes. The population of innovators has increased at very high rates in all countries and especially in Italy, the UK, Japan and France, while remaining constant in Switzerland and Denmark.

Similarly, the average number of patents per firm, which one can use as an index of research output, has increased over time in all countries except Japan, the UK and Italy (see Table 6.1). One also observes a tendency towards increasing differentiation across countries in their patterns of innovative activities in genetic engineering, either as a result of increases in the research output of firms, as in Switzerland, Germany, the Netherlands

Table 6.1 Changes in EPO patents between 1978–86 and 1987–93

Country	Per cent change in no. of applications/firm	Per cent change in total patent applications	Patent applications per firm (1978–86)	Patent applications per firm (1987–93)
US	0.30	0.40	3.20	3.40
Japan	0.60	0.56	2.89	2.80
Germany	0.03	0.87	2.80	5.12
UK	0.84	0.73	2.50	2.35
France	0.49	0.77	2.48	2.95
Switzerland	0.00	0.98	3.09	6.14
Netherlands	0.45	1.04	2.75	3.86
Denmark	−0.29	0.69	2.29	3.85
Italy	2.1	2.70	2.56	2.20

Source: European Patent Office.

and Denmark, or as an expansion of the total number of innovators, as in France and the US. The first case could be called a 'deepening' pattern of innovative activities (Malerba and Orsenigo, 1995, 1996), while the second could be called a 'widening' pattern of innovation.

Turning to the evolution of innovators themselves, a stable group of innovators is present in all countries throughout the period considered. Indeed in most countries, the ranking of innovators changed very little between the two periods 1978–86 and 1987–93. In the US, there were both new entries to this group of major innovators and some significant changes in the hierarchy of companies within this group. Significantly, this was as much the case for the DBFs as the large companies. At the same time, however, a core group of persistent innovators is easily identifiable and includes both DBFs and large, established companies. A similar pattern emerged for Japan, although there are no DBFs among the main innovators. The large European and Japanese companies do not appear to have fared particularly badly when compared with firms in the US. The technological lead of the US appears to be linked, in this respect, less to the absolute level of innovative activities, as measured by the number of EPO patent applications, than to the existence of a much larger number of companies that are involved in biotechnology R&D. The 20 firms with the largest number of EPO patent applications include eight from the US, three from Japan and three from Germany. The number of European firms patenting had also increased significantly by the second period.

Along with the existence of this group of stable, persistent innovators, the industry is characterized by a great deal of entry and exit outside of the core group of firms, suggesting that the industry is still very much in a period of development and turbulence, as would be expected of a young industry such as biotechnology.

The role of the DBF is also significantly different by country. In the US, DBFs play a substantial role, with a number of companies included in the top ten innovators. DBFs are also significant sources of innovation in the UK, in France and in the Netherlands. Their contribution is negligible in Japan, Germany, Switzerland, Denmark and Italy. In these latter countries, established firms are by far the most important innovators. Conversely, the role of incumbents is less important, though always significant, in the US and above all in France, where innovative activities tend to be centred around the system of public research. The public research system also plays an important role in other European countries, most notably the UK, while its contribution is relatively low in Denmark, Italy and Switzerland.

STRATEGIC ALLIANCES AND COLLABORATIVE NETWORKS

An interesting feature of the biotechnology industry is the enormous expansion in strategic alliances between large and small companies. Many of these alliances relate specifically to exchanges of technology, or to joint R&D projects, as firms attempt to develop and expand their technological expertise. Network analysis is used to examine the evolution of these relationships between large and small firms.

Two sources of data are used: the Cooperative Agreements and Technology Indicators (CATI) database and Bioscan. The former contains information on over 10,000 cooperative agreements involving 4,000 different parent companies (Hagedoorn and Huibers, 1995),[3] and is used to study the evolution of the R&D network in three European countries: Italy, the Netherlands and the UK. The Bioscan dataset is used primarily to compare and contrast the larger European network with that of the US, referring back to our main objective of understanding the role of the DBF and its contribution to the development of competitiveness in biotechnology.

The Network in Selected European Countries

Analysis of the CATI data shows that the total number of strategic alliances in biotechnology has increased enormously since the 1970s, except for a decline between 1987 and 1991. Joint R&D is the primary form of cooperation between companies in the three countries analysed, followed by equity joint ventures. As expected, the alliances in the three countries tend to be concentrated in national industries with strong technological competences, such as pharmaceutical and medical technologies in the UK and agro-biotech in the Netherlands, whereas Italy is fairly equally divided between the two, with considerable activity in fine chemicals as well. The total number of alliances is greatest in the UK, with the Netherlands a close second and Italy a distant third (Table 6.2).

An examination of the network of alliances in each country showed that the Netherlands and Italy have, respectively, the densest and most centralized network and the least dense and centralized network. In general, the networks tend to concentrate around a few core companies. Their alliances also tend to be 'European' in that they link up primarily with firms in other European countries and in particular with companies in the same country. The UK also shows a high propensity to link up with companies in the US, while in general collaboration with Japanese companies tends to be low.

Table 6.2　Biotechnology alliances in selected countries, 1970–93
　　　　　(percentage of the total)

Country	Total	Intra[1]	Inter[2]
Italy	37	1	36
	(2.8)	(2.7)	(97.3)
United Kingdom	159	23	136
	(12.1)	(14.5)	(85.5)
Netherlands	116	36	80
	(8.8)	(31.0)	(69.0)
Total (World)	1317		
	(100)		

Notes:
1. All partners involved originate from the same country.
2. At least one partner in the alliance originates from a foreign country.

Source:　MERIT–CATI database.

The European and US Networks

An analysis of the larger European network and a comparison with that of the US shows several interesting differences and similarities. The European network emerged later in time and began under very different initial conditions. The US network is six times the size of the European network and three times as dense (that is, 48.5 per cent of US alliances are between firms in the US, whereas in the case of Europe this figure is 15.4 per cent). The European network depends heavily on the American one, with 83 per cent of European alliances being made with US firms and 7 per cent with Japanese firms, whereas only 61 per cent of US firm alliances are with European firms and 34 per cent are with Japan. The two networks also differ in terms of government involvement in biotechnology R&D, with the US government accounting for 11 per cent of biotechnology agreements compared with European government involvement in only 2 per cent of alliances in Europe.

　　An analysis of the networks over time also shows interesting differences. One notes the almost complete absence of DBFs formed in the period 1975–80 in the European network. The relative importance of freestanding firms[4] in the European network also tends to be greater than in the US, as is the number of technology alliances in which large incumbents are involved. Incumbents remain at the centre of the European network and link with second- and third-generation DBFs (formed in 1980–85 and after 1985, respectively). Only a small number of first-generation biotechnology firms link primarily with universities, and these appear to be separated from the other companies. In contrast, in the US network, the first-generation DBFs, as well as incumbents, maintain strong relationships with all subsequent generations of firms. Over time the patterns of relationships formed by American first-generation DBFs becomes quite similar to those formed by the incumbents. The same pattern is noticeable in the European network, although in the European case it is especially noticeable with the second group of entrants.

Thus a kind of 'life cycle' seems to characterize the evolution of the network, with each generation of entrants following similar patterns of growth and relationships within the network. In the beginning, new entrants depend strongly on universities and public research institutes. They also appear to establish linkages with the oldest firms in the industry. Over time, however, their relationships with universities decline and they become increasingly similar to the previous generation of companies.

The results confirm that the network of collaborations has grown significantly over time both in the US and, with a time lag, in Europe. At the same time, the centrality of the networks has increased as well, suggesting that the networks increasingly adopt a 'vertical' or hierarchical structure, with an expanding and turbulent periphery. There appear to be strong first-mover advantages, with early entrants becoming increasingly central to the network. The first-generation DBFs become increasingly indistinguishable from the incumbents in terms of the structure of their agreements with other network participants. As the network becomes more centralized in this way, it becomes harder for new entrants to grow and challenge the core firms. Furthermore, European DBFs have increasingly to compete directly with American DBFs in order to maintain their position or to enter the network at all.

NATIONAL STUDIES

In order to examine the process of innovation in biotechnology in the European network, national biotechnology surveys followed by in-depth company and institutional interviews were conducted in Italy, the Netherlands and the UK. While patent and network analyses help to present a general overview of the market and institutional structure, the in-depth interviews provide an analysis of the difficulties and successes of individual institutions involved in innovation. Going back to one of the original questions posed in this chapter, the interviews were used to study the role of the DBF within the European framework. Below, we present some comparisons across the three countries surveyed.

The Interviews

In general, the interviews attempted to cover all the various actors involved in biotechnology R&D in each country, including public sector research institutions, universities, research and industrial associations, established incumbent firms active in biotechnology R&D and DBFs, where present. In the case of the Netherlands and the UK, the interviewed companies and institutions were selected from the respondents to a survey questionnaire. The survey identified companies that were active in third-generation biotechnology research, had developed any biotechnology-related products and had formal or informal collaborations with other companies or research institutions. This method also enabled us to ensure that the group of companies and institutions interviewed was representative of the entire research community and also allowed us to identify sub-sectors in which innovative activity was concentrated. Thus a larger percentage of British firms interviewed were from the pharmaceutical field than in the Netherlands, where innovation is focused on agricultural biotechnology. An effort was also made to concentrate on the role of the DBF and its relationship to the research community. In total, 46 firms and institutions were interviewed across all three countries, including private and public sector firms and research institutions (Table 6.3).

Table 6.3　Participating companies/institutions[1]

	Italy	Netherlands	United Kingdom
Public sector	6	3	5
Private sector	13[a]	8	13[b]
Pharma/medical	11	4	8
Agro-biotech	1	4	5
Fine chemicals	1	–	–
Other	1	–	2
Total (companies and institutions)	19	11	18

Notes:
a Three firms engaged in more than one area of R&D.
b Two firms engaged in more than one area of R&D.
1 The total number of firms in the table add up to more than 46 because of overlaps in research activities.

Of the companies interviewed in Italy, 11 were active in the field of therapeutics, three in diagnostics, one in fine chemicals, one in agricultural biotechnology and one was an engineering society for the design and rationalization of biotechnology plants and/or laboratories. Of these companies, however, two firms had ceased all biotechnology activities since 1994, while one could be classified as a supplier firm. None could be classified as a DBF.

In the Netherlands, four of the eight firms interviewed were in the pharma/medical field, while the other four were involved in agricultural biotechnology. This distribution approximates the survey results that found that of the 30 Dutch firms that are active in genetic engineering research, approximately half fall in the agro-biotech sector. Two of the agro-biotech firms are DBFs, one was established by a larger firm as a research subsidiary, and the fourth is a small or medium-sized firm that has added capabilities in molecular biology and genetic engineering to its existing R&D programme.

Of the 12 companies interviewed in the UK, six were involved in biotechnology R&D in the pharmaceutical sector, two were small diagnostics companies, three were agricultural companies and one was an environmental company.[5] Of the pharmaceutical companies, two were large while the rest were specialized biotechnology companies, while in agriculture, two were associated with large companies, being either part of, or closely allied with, a large company. The third agricultural company was independent and sought out alliances with other R&D-based companies for genetic engineering technologies, while its own R&D was more concentrated on downstream applications in plant biotechnology.

The goals of the interviews were twofold: first, to identify the research and market strategies of firms and the effect of these strategies on their innovative and competitive activities. The second was to study their response to their particular external environment, including government support for research, intellectual property rights and regulation. In general, the key focus was the 'evolution' of biotechnology in Europe, and the role of research and marketing strategies and the external environment in the successful development of the European biotechnology network.

Research Strategies

The interview results showed that DBFs could be classified into two main groups with considerably different research strategies. Research-driven firms focus on leading-edge technologies and build up strong patent portfolios and a skilled technical staff. In contrast, the application-driven firms concentrate on the use of relatively familiar and generic technologies that can be adapted to solve specific problems. In other words, research-driven firms concentrate on research in new technologies and on pushing out the technology frontier, whereas application-driven firms concentrate on developing products using incremental improvements in technology. The goals of the research-driven companies therefore tend to be the development of new products based on radical new techniques which implies research of a long-term nature. The application-driven company emphasizes the development of products over a shorter term.

Several research-driven DBFs[6] faced the problem that their research projects were too long term and costly. Short-term applications and products often had to be found in order to finance their long-term research. In most cases, however, even though short-term applications had to be found, this did not appear to dissuade many companies from their original goals, including the long-term research projects they had started out with. In the case of the multinationals and other non-DBF firms, their strategies have been very much dominated by efforts to incorporate biotechnology research into their existing R&D programmes by acquiring DBFs, if necessary, or through collaborative research.

Market Strategies

Although several of the firms interviewed were formed by individuals in the research community, all have had to face changes in their marketing conditions, and their strategies have had to be adapted to these changing conditions. Some of these changing conditions arose as the company moved from the research stage into downstream product development, where the problems related to marketing are considerably different to those in the early stages of research.

For the DBFs, especially those that are research driven, the immediate as well as long-term strategy is to obtain funding for R&D before a marketable product is ready. The companies have done this through a variety of sources, including government funding or funding from National Research Councils, private placements, venture capital and from selling a partial interest in a project to another firm. In the longer run, companies have tended to seek funding through public offerings, although this has often proved difficult for a number of reasons elaborated below. Another method that has been used quite successfully by a few research-driven companies is to fund their R&D by licensing out patented products or technologies and by developing strategic alliances with other companies. As a number of research-driven companies now move from the research stage to the production and marketing of new products, they will be faced with the question of whether to try and increase vertical integration within the company by producing and marketing their products. The alternative is to license their products to someone else and to concentrate on research rather than development. With a couple of exceptions, it seems highly unlikely that most research-driven firms will become fully integrated.

The large multinationals have experienced relatively little change in their marketing strategies since they have always pursued an integrated policy spanning research, testing, production and marketing. The major change for these firms is the growth of their technology alliances with small biotechnology companies.

The public sector has experienced a few changes in recent years, especially due to changes in its funding and its relationship with downstream applied research carried out by biotechnology companies and multinationals. Funding in general, and especially public sector funding, has become harder to come by and universities often find themselves competing with the private sector for the same research funds. The multinationals continue to fund universities but their collaborations with DBFs have also deepened. The strategy of universities has had to adapt to such changes in their traditional sources of funding. Many universities, for example, have established consultancy services and have tried to obtain royalties from patent licensing. Both have helped universities to expand their formal and informal relationships with biotechnology companies, but in the Netherlands, at least, universities have yet to earn very much from royalties.

Collaboration

As biotechnology has become more established, the relationships between the various players, especially the universities, multinationals and DBFs, have become more interdependent. In developing these collaborative links, it is clear that each of the three players has very different interests, but the complementary skills that they bring into their collaborations have served to deepen these relationships in recent years and, if anything, make them more complex.

In general, all firms, be they large MNCs or small DBFs, tend to maintain close links with universities and public sector research institutions. The most obvious reason for this is access to basic knowledge and technical capabilities.

Most DBFs acknowledge the importance of maintaining contacts with the public research sector, either on a general level or on a more project-specific basis, and stress the importance of these contacts to maintain their technological lead or to catch up with technological leaders. Specific project funding provided to universities also helps to keep in-house research costs down for many companies, since they can use the expertise and equipment provided by universities rather than having to invest in it themselves. Companies also appear to prefer project-specific funding in collaborations with the public sector because, according to them, it helps the academic to focus on the goals of the particular project rather than pursuing interesting ideas with no commercial applicability.

The MNCs have continued their collaboration with universities, mainly through project funding and also via some funding for research and training programmes. From their earlier, hesitant attitude towards biotechnology, several MNCs have developed in-house technical capabilities through collaboration with DBFs. Nevertheless, collaboration has continued, especially in new techniques developed by DBFs which continue to have an edge in new technologies.[7] Several firms also provide funding for 'blue skies' research, although this is becoming much rarer as companies cut back on their R&D budgets.

The research-driven DBFs therefore have increasingly been sought out by the multinationals for their technological capabilities,[8] especially as products developed by the former reach the production and marketing stage. Many of the DBFs are able to take products up to stage II or III clinical trials, after which the cost of production and marketing becomes prohibitive for them. They therefore prefer to license the product to a multinational in return for royalties which enable them to raise funds to continue their research. In the case of the application-driven and niche market companies, there is a tendency to collaborate with other companies of the same or similar size for manufacturing and marketing purposes as well as some technology alliances. The tendency to develop relationships with other firms of a similar size partly reflects a risk aversion on the part of these firms and partly a fear of being taken over by large DBFs or MNCs.

Thus as the technology develops, strategic alliances between the public and private sectors and within the private sector have increased. Each partner brings a complementary asset into the alliance, with the collaborations changing in nature and partnership as the technology develops. This evolution over time is clearest in the alliances formed by the DBF, with its focus shifting somewhat from the university or research institution to the multinational as it moves from the research stage into product development. The multinational similarly finds it attractive to license products developed by the DBF which it is also able to market more effectively and rapidly than the DBF. The DBF also continues to be an attractive source of applied knowledge. The university, in turn, provides the basic scientific knowledge which is rapidly changing biotechnology into an important new technology.

The Institutional Framework

The institutional framework that the company or university develops is often crucial to its development and determines its evolution and survival in the long run. As the DBF moves towards product development and marketing, its institutional requirements also change. Questions about property rights, regulations and long-term financing become more important and often determine the success of a particular company or technology.

Patenting appears to have become an important factor in the competitiveness of most of the companies interviewed. Having intellectual property rights, many companies argue, strengthens their competitive position, especially *vis-à-vis* the multinationals. It also makes it easier for them to find partners to collaborate with, both because they have a proprietary technology that can be licensed in return for royalty payments, and also because the patented technology or product gives the company clear ownership over the product in any collaboration. Even in agriculture, where hands-on applied and tacit knowledge is often more important than codified knowledge, companies acknowledged the importance of patenting in biotechnology. Several companies therefore expressed disappointment with the failure of the European Parliament to adopt the European patent directive, and hoped that a decision could soon be reached on a Europe-wide patent framework. The situation as it exists today, it was felt above all, conveys a negative image to the world of a Europe that cannot agree on this issue.

Among the universities and institutions in the public sector, the number of patent applications, and certainly the awareness of the importance of patenting, has grown in the last decade or so. Concern was, however, expressed about the potential conflict between the need to patent (and therefore to withhold information from the public domain until the patent is published) and the need to publish quickly in order to release information into the public domain, which is what is usually expected of an academic.

There was relatively less universal agreement on the issue of regulation. In general, the problem appeared to lie not so much in the regulation of R&D, but in the regulatory requirements concerning product testing and marketing. Companies in the UK, for example, felt that regulation in the UK was more than adequate and that regulatory requirements in some other European countries were too stringent. In the Netherlands it was felt, especially by firms involved in medical and pharmaceutical biotechnology, that there were no major differences between Europe and the US in terms of regulatory requirements. In fact, they felt that any new product took longer to introduce in the US market than in

Europe. However, they argued that it would be useful to streamline the process further, and several companies regularly lobbied their regulatory authorities to improve the system. In Italy, companies have made the adjustments required of them by the recent EC directives which set a minimum standard. However, firms in agricultural biotechnology felt that there was an urgent need to increase and systematize regulation in all three countries in order to increase consumer confidence in the industry and to permit firms to market genetically engineered products and thereby recoup their research investments.

Finally, in the case of financing, companies in general have not had great difficulty in raising funding. There were a few cases where initial funding was difficult to come by, but in general it was felt that if the ideas and the technologies were sound, investors would be willing to invest in the company. Several of the companies that were formed in the 1980s have now even gone public to increase funding for their R&D. Initially their public offerings were made on the American market, where alternative sources of funding, such as the National Association of Securities Dealers Automated Quotation (NASDAQ), were especially attractive. Major stock exchanges in Europe, such as the London Stock Exchange, had requirements that most biotechnology companies could not meet and so most early funding was raised through NASDAQ. Many companies expressed hope that the European equivalent of NASDAQ, EASDAQ, would function as efficiently as its American counterpart, and several have also made public offerings at the London Stock Exchange since it modified its rules to accommodate the needs of new technology companies.

CONCLUSIONS

The in-depth company interviews, aided by the patent and network analysis, showed that biotechnology has developed in a very individualistic manner across European countries. Its development, as expected, is closely related to the strengths and weaknesses of the institutional frameworks of each country. The adaptability of these institutional frameworks is also crucial in responding to the needs of a changing technology. Nevertheless, despite these differences, we can use these analyses to suggest a few general conclusions.

First, when compared with the US, Europe finds itself a latecomer to biotechnology and continues to lag behind the US in absolute terms. However, the picture is highly differentiated across countries in Europe, and in recent years there have been indications of significant improvements and success stories in both the UK and the Netherlands.

Second, while the DBF has played a central role in the commercialization of biotechnology in the US, its role has been less important in Europe in general and also in the countries analysed in this study, especially in Italy. In Europe, biotechnology research has been driven mainly by large, existing corporations and by the public sector research system. However, even the large corporation appears to have lagged behind when compared with its American counterpart, with a few noticeable exceptions such as those European multinationals which started building up their biotechnology capability at an early date and have built strong networks with small and large companies and universities in order to broaden their base (Sharp, forthcoming).

Although the emergence of the DBF was slower in Europe, it is now a growing force, especially in countries such as the UK and, to a lesser extent, the Netherlands, where it is now more closely involved in the biotechnology networks of these countries. Italy is conspicuous in that it almost completely lacks DBFs. Results from the network analysis seem to show, however, that the European DBF is significantly different from its American counterpart. Even in those cases where they have emerged successfully, the European DBFs do not resemble American DBFs, being much more closely linked to the public sector research system and to large corporations. In both the Netherlands and the UK, this study found, particularly through the in-depth interviews, that while DBFs perform a valuable role in furthering the level of knowledge, it is likely that their function could be performed by direct contacts between large firms and public sector research institutions. Furthermore, those firms that are successful in marketing their products and in capturing market share are likely to be taken over by large firms or become part of a larger consortium of companies. Current niche market companies are likely to remain independent, both because their markets are too small to attract large firms and because their success partially depends on close, often informal and personal collaboration with the public research sector. Their role is, however, likely to be confined to niche markets, although not necessarily in the same product areas as at present.

The exception to this is a small group of companies in the UK especially, which do function as system integrators and perhaps come closest to the US model in Europe. These firms may be in a position to become fully integrated pharmaceutical companies or remain in the market as independent biotechnology companies, although they are still at a relatively early stage of development and much depends on whether they are successful in bringing products to market in the next few years. Much also depends on the ability of these companies to develop key technologies independently of the large multinationals.

The structure of the collaborative network in Europe tells a similar story and looks quite different from the American case. While its growth follows structural paths similar to those taken by the US, it is still much less dense than in the US and strongly oriented towards the latter. In other words, the European network is still in its infancy, with relatively self-contained national sub-networks and, if anything, linked to the US instead of other European countries. The expansion of local networks, especially in the UK, may however generate a distinct European network in the future. The relatively minor role played by DBFs in Europe seems to be a function of different variables. The results of our research point to the lower absolute levels of scientific research in universities and to the structure of the academic system which discourage researchers from moving between academia and the private sector, whereas financial constraints do not appear to have played a significant role.

Thus we come to our key question on the future competitiveness of European biotechnology and the policy measures required of national governments and the European Commission. Our research suggests that in a science-based technology such as biotechnology, there are significant first-mover advantages and therefore catching up is not likely and is certainly not an automatic process. However, this does not imply that some substantial catching up is not possible, especially in specific niches. How this can be achieved raises some important questions about the nature of the innovation process, the role of the DBF in innovation and the goals of governments in facilitating this process of innovation.

DBFs have played a fundamental role in the US as explorers of technological opportunities and facilitators of innovation. They have played an important bridging function between university research and the market. In contrast, there have been far fewer DBFs in Europe, while at the same time European industry lags behind the technical expertise of American firms. The question for European policy makers is whether DBFs play a crucial role in the development of biotechnology (or, similarly, if small, dedicated high technology firms are essential to the development of any new science-based technology) and whether further policy support for DBFs will assist European industry in catching up with the technological leaders.

One possibility is that the 'window of opportunity' for supporting DBFs is closing. This is shown both in the US and in Europe by the rapid rate at which successful DBFs are bought out by large MNCs. Other DBFs have become very successful and have grown into vertically integrated firms. While still based in biotechnology, they are no longer small, and are evolving into MNCs. However, there is still considerable activity occurring at the level of small DBFs, and therefore they are likely to play an important role for some time in the future.

At the same time, large European MNCs are capable of bypassing European DBFs and forming direct links with the public research system or alliances with firms of all sizes, both within Europe but particularly in the US, that have valuable technical expertise. This suggests that any linear view of innovation in this sector, whereby DBFs fill an essential stage between basic research conducted at universities and the applied and market-oriented research performed by large firms, is misplaced. The evolution of the alliance network suggests instead that DBFs have performed, and are increasingly performing, a role of exploration rather than simple bridging. Moreover, innovative activities, both within firms and within the network, do not appear to be easily separable into vertical stages, going from science to production and marketing. If anything, the division of labour (and therefore cooperation) is generated by the complexity of, and the rapidity of progress of, the knowledge base.

The paucity of European DBFs, the growing technical capabilities of large European firms and the integrated nature of the biotechnology sector suggest several policy options. It is probably too late for Europe to catch up with the US through a flurry of new DBF entrants. Much of the future of European biotechnology capabilities lies with existing DBFs and with large MNCs. However, policies to support new technology firms of any kind should be introduced, not only because this should have some positive effects for biotechnology, but also because it may assist the development of future new technologies that lie over the horizon. Second, policies should encourage integration of the knowledge base through strengthening the technical capabilities of all the various actors – of which one of the most important is the public research sector. Third, some sub-fields of biotechnology, for example the agro-biotech sector, have evolved to the stage where future benefits will depend on the diffusion of the technology into existing firms that largely use conventional technologies. This diffusion of technical capabilities needs to be encouraged. Possible policy options include information programmes, the strengthening of biotechnology capabilities at regional universities and technical institutes, and a careful evaluation of the patent and licensing system to ensure that conventional firms will not be completely shut out from biotechnological applications by strong patent families held by MNCs and DBFs.

NOTES

1. This chapter is based on a study (Acharya, Arundel and Orsenigo, 1996) financed by the BIOTECH Programme of the European Commission, DG XII. We would like to thank J. Hagedoorn, S. Huibers, M. Riccaboni, F. Pammoli and L. Rossi for their assistance in

researching and preparing the original report. The study on which this chapter is based commenced when Rohini Acharya was a researcher at MERIT, Maastricht and completed when she was Senior Research Fellow at the Royal Institute of International Affairs. The views expressed here are those of the author and not of her present organization.

2. A 'biotechnology' patent can be attributed to a number of different technology classes leading to an underestimation or overestimation of the number of patents. Using a relatively narrow class such as C12N attempts to overcome part of this problem by defining more precisely what we mean by biotechnology.

3. Cooperative agreements in this case are defined as common interests between independent industrial partners which are not connected through majority ownership. The CATI database includes only those inter-firm agreements that concern arrangements relating to technology transfer or joint research, that is, alliances relating to innovation specifically.

4. Companies with no collaborative agreements.

5. Four other environmental companies were approached for an interview, but the request was either turned down or no response was received.

6. The discussion in this section only refers to firms in the Netherlands and the UK because none of the firms in Italy can be classified as DBFs.

7. Senker and Sharp (1997) also point out that while the MNC has developed in-house capabilities in biotechnology through collaboration with a DBF, one of the objectives of maintaining collaborations with DBFs is to continue to learn about new techniques being developed by them. One large pharmaceutical MNC interviewed for the purposes of this present study also pointed out that while biotechnology was an important new technology, it remained an *addition* to older techniques used in drug discovery. The company therefore continued to see collaboration with DBFs as an important source of information about the new techniques being developed in the field of biotechnology which the company could then seek to acquire if they proved useful and complementary to its own research agenda.

8. Senker and Sharp (1997) moreover point out that collaboration with large MNCs has given DBFs credibility. This has helped them to develop further collaborations and to raise additional funds, for example from venture capital companies and from public offerings on the stock market.

REFERENCES

Acharya, R., A. Arundel and L. Orsenigo (1996), *The Evolving Structure of the Biotechnology Industry and its Future Competitiveness*, Final Report for the Biotechnology Programme (BIOTECH) of the European Community, DG XII, Maastricht: MERIT, University of Limburg.

Arora, A. and A. Gambardella (1990), 'Complementarity and external linkage: the strategies of the large firms in biotechnology', *Journal of Industrial Economics,* **38**(4), 361–79.

Gambardella, A. (1995), *Science and Innovation in the US Pharmaceutical Industry*, Cambridge: Cambridge University Press.

Hagedoorn, J. and S. Huibers (1995), *The Evolving Structure of the Biotechnology Industry and its Future Competitiveness: Strategic Alliances*, Maastricht: MERIT, University of Limburg.

Henderson, R. (1994), 'The evolution of integrative competence: innovation in cardiovascular drug discovery', *Industrial and Corporate Change*, **3** (3), 607–30.

Klepper, S. (1992), *Entry, Exit and Innovation over the Product Life Cycle: The Dynamics of First Mover Advantages, Declining Product Innovation and Market Failure*, paper presented at the International J.A. Schumpeter Society, Kyoto, August.

Malerba, F. and L. Orsenigo (1995), 'Schumpeterian patterns of innovation', *Cambridge Journal of Economics*, **19**(1), 47–65.

Malerba, F. and L. Orsenigo (1996), 'Schumpeterian patterns of innovation are technology-specific', *Research Policy*, **25**(3), 451–78.

Orsenigo, L. (1989), *The Emergence of Biotechnology*, London: Pinter Publishers.

Pisano, G. (1991), 'The governance of innovation: vertical integration and collaborative arrangements in the biotechnology industry', *Research Policy*, **20**(3), 237–47.

Senker, J. and M. Sharp (1997), 'Organizational learning in cooperative alliances: some case studies from biotechnology', *Technology Analysis and Strategic Management*, **9**(1), 35–51.

Sharp, M. (1995), *The New Biotechnology: European Governments in Search of a Strategy*, Sussex European Papers, Brighton: University of Sussex.

Sharp, M. (forthcoming), 'The Science of Nations: European Multinationals and American Biotechnology', *International Journal of Technology Management* (Biotechnology Review).

7. Biotechnology and Europe's chemical/pharmaceutical multinationals

Jacqueline Senker, Pierre-Benoît Joly
and **Michael Reinhard**

INTRODUCTION

Europe provides the home base for many of the world's leading chemical and pharmaceutical multinational companies. The success of this industry has been built on mastery of its core technology, synthetic organic chemistry. Recognizing the significance of developments in biotechnology to their continued competitive success, companies have taken steps to acquire new biotechnology capabilities. These efforts have been paralleled by national and European Union (EU) policies to build up the science base in biotechnology, to encourage technology transfer and to regulate biotechnology. However, the leading edge of research in biotechnology has remained in the US, where the emergence of a dynamic new sector based on small specialist research firms closely linked to academia has led to what can only be described as an 'explosion' of the inter-related science and technology base.

In an effort to access American knowledge and capabilities, many Europe-based companies have set up or extended their US laboratories and negotiated contracts with US academic laboratories and/or dedicated biotechnology firms (DBFs). These same companies have simultaneously retained their established links with their indigenous science bases and forged new linkages in the area of the life sciences. Nevertheless, it is generally acknowledged that, with the exception of the UK, Europe has fallen behind US capabilities. In addition, Europe has failed to develop the dynamic small firm sector that is such a feature of the US scene (Sharp, Thomas and Martin, 1993).

The overall result of these developments means that while European-owned multinationals have retained their competitive edge and built up the necessary capabilities in this area, it is not clear that Europe itself (in a geographic sense) is acquiring the same skills and capabilities in biotechnology and could be falling behind. The effects on European competence depend on the extent to which the multinational companies are repatriating to their domestic laboratories the knowledge, skills and capabilities built up in the US. This chapter is based on a study which investigated this issue by looking at the organization and management of biotechnology R&D by Europe's leading chemical/ pharmaceutical multinational companies, and the relationship between their US and European research efforts (Senker, Joly and Reinhard, 1996).[1] The study involved ten in-depth case studies of leading German, French and British chemical/pharmaceutical multinationals, based on semi-structured interviews with senior managers responsible for biotechnology research in the home country and in the US. It explored:

1. The number of qualified scientists and engineers (QSEs) working on biotechnology issues in home and US laboratories and how they were recruited.
2. The nature, focus and type of biotechnology R&D in companies' home and overseas laboratories.
3. Their methods for building up and diffusing biotechnology capabilities in and between home and overseas laboratories, including collaborations with university research and DBFs.
4. The regulatory environment, scientific capabilities or other factors influencing the location of company biotechnology research in the US.
5. The effect of overseas research on European biotechnology capabilities.

NATURE AND LOCATION OF BIOTECHNOLOGY ACTIVITIES

Of the ten case study companies, half apply biotechnology to a broad range of chemical and pharmaceutical businesses; the other half are either involved only in pharmaceuticals or apply biotechnology mainly to their pharmaceutical business. As shown in Table 7.1, the major application of biotechnology is to the health and diagnostics areas. All the interviews in Europe provided information about companies' use of biotechnology in health; companies were rather guarded about their application of biotechnology to seeds and plant protection. We have information on these two areas from three companies only and none of these provided access to their US R&D facilities. Thus our US interviews were mainly with the health divisions of the companies concerned and the results are biased towards this application.

Table 7.1 Focus of companies' biotechnology activities

Company	Health	Diagnostics	Food/Seeds	Plant Protection	Other*
A	X	X	X	X	X
B	X	X	X	X	–
C	X	–	X	X	X
D	X	–	–	X	–
E	X	X	–	X	X
F	X	–	–	–	–
G	X	X	–	–	X
H	X	X	–	–	–
I	X	X	–	–	–
J	X	–	–	–	–

Notes: *Businesses such as fine chemicals or animal health.

All the companies began to explore the potential applications of biotechnology by the late 1970s or early 1980s, or even earlier, and first applied biotechnology to their research activities in Europe. Most of the companies have now extended the application of biotechnology to their US laboratories, with two exceptions. Company G has decided to concentrate its biotechnology efforts at home in Europe. Company H also goes against the trend by applying biotechnology only to its diagnostics business in the US. It has made a strategic decision not to get involved in pharmaceutical biotechnology in the US, because the use of traditional techniques to identify new molecules has been so successful that it has more than enough new drugs in the development pipeline.

Two companies had long-established US subsidiaries and seven acquired US firms during the period 1972–90. Few of these acquisitions were involved in R&D, but one had biotechnology expertise and two had production capabilities in second-generation biotechnology. By the early 1980s, biotechnology was being applied in companies' existing US laboratories and in six newly established laboratories. In the late 1980s, the tenth company merged with a US company; both had similar competences in biotechnology.

Two companies increased their US research efforts deliberately to tap into strong US biotechnology research both in the universities and in DBFs, and one German company set up both biotechnology research and production in the US as a direct result of restrictive implementation of gene law by local *Länder* officials. In agriculture, biotechnology research in the US is partly explained by the need to carry out field trials near the main market, primarily for climatic reasons. But one company's facilities were created to access scientific competences which, at the time, were available only in the US. These companies, however, do not represent the norm.

The majority of companies in pharmaceuticals increased their US R&D in order to enter or reinforce their position in the US market, the largest pharmaceutical market in the world. It is necessary for companies which regard themselves as global players to undertake R&D in all their major markets. Nonetheless, the establishment of US facilities also had another effect. Some European laboratories were late in taking the genetic engineering revolution seriously. Inertia resulted from 'old guard' pharmacologists driving the research agenda. New US laboratories were set up at about the time that biotechnology began to be exploited in pharmaceutical research, and biotechnology often diffused through the new US laboratories more quickly than in Europe. Sometimes, the US laboratories demonstrated the power of the technology to such good effect that biotechnology became more fully integrated into European research efforts.

EMPLOYMENT OF BIOTECHNOLOGY QSEs

Companies were asked how many R&D employees they had in their laboratories with doctoral or post-doctoral qualifications who were working on issues which fall into the category of biotechnology. Companies differed in their interpretation of what is meant by 'biotechnology' and who to count as QSEs; some included technicians and others excluded them. Difficulty was also created when companies did not think of their researchers in a 'biotechnology' category, with some suggesting that there was now such widespread diffusion of biotechnology techniques throughout their laboratories that it was difficult to give a meaningful answer. The data provided have been analysed to make them comparable between companies, by calculating the percentage of companies' biotechnology QSEs in various locations throughout the world. Given the difficulties in data collection, and the bias which may have been introduced by the sample of companies selected for our study, our results must be interpreted with caution. Table 7.2 shows that, on average, home laboratories have 59 per cent of biotechnology research staff, US laboratories 35 per cent, and the remaining 6 per cent are in laboratories in the rest of the world (the major concentrations being about 2 per cent in Latin America for field trials of crops, 2 per cent in Japan for screening and 1 per cent in Australia for pharmaceutical research).

There is some difference between regions when these percentages are disaggregated between pharmaceuticals and plants/seeds. In pharmaceu-

Table 7.2   Percentage of companies' biotechnology research by location (by numbers of research staff)

Country/Region	Overall %	Pharmaceuticals %	Plants/Seeds %
Europe	59	42	16
US	35	21	14
Rest of World	6	3	3

ticals, the US proportion of total biotechnology QSEs is half the proportion of that in European laboratories. In plants/seeds the proportions in both locations are very similar.

Within Europe, UK companies have the highest proportion of these biotechnology QSEs (35 per cent), followed by France (29 per cent), Germany (22 per cent) and Switzerland (12 per cent); there are also small groups in Belgium, Italy and Spain.

Each laboratory recruits researchers from the locally available pool of recruits. The main criterion affecting recruitment is the competence of the people concerned. Two British companies mentioned that the competition for skilled biotechnology researchers is greater in the UK than in the US, and the former has a smaller pool of expertise in specific areas. Lack of specialists in the UK may lead to certain types of work being carried out in the US, for instance bio-informatics. Another company reported that biotechnology research in the US laboratory might be increased at the expense of European facilities, because it is easier to attract high calibre people from the US training system, both in terms of the numbers available and of the expertise available. Microbial and viral research used to be the responsibility of the European laboratory, but they have been moved to the US where the company can recruit people with expertise in these areas. Reductions in microbiology training worldwide have caused a similar shift of research to US laboratories.

The US laboratories have no problems in recruiting biotechnology staff and mainly rely on personal networks for all but the most senior positions. The general lack of recruitment problems in the US is ascribed to the 'rich' US research environment: 'All a scientist looks for is good peers and resources to do research and that is available [here]'. Some laboratories recruit a tiny proportion of senior managers from Europe, but most research staff are US born or trained. 'US trained' reflects the fact that a great many post-doctoral researchers in the US come from Asia and Europe, and the QSEs recruited reflect this trend. Research staff who are European by origin had all done post-doctoral research in US universities and often these

European researchers are better than their US peers, because, 'they were top of their class [in Europe] and therefore got into the top labs in the US'. In the words of one of the senior managers interviewed: 'the difference that this US training gives is to make researchers more driven, more aggressive than their European-trained counterparts'.

There was a divergence of views on the relative advantages of post-graduate training in various countries. A senior company manager in Europe thought that one of the major problems with the European system of education was the advanced age when studies were completed. He had the impression that Americans get their first post-doctoral experience when three to four years younger than their European counterparts. The lack of uniformity in the European training system was reflected in the comments of a European senior manager in a US laboratory. He perceived that US researchers have longer postgraduate and broader undergraduate training than in the UK. Thus US students are both properly trained and mature when they complete their PhDs around the age of 27, unlike their British counterparts who can be three years younger. Another European manager contrasted US, French and German training. In the US and France doctoral programmes are completed by the time students are 24 or 25 years of age; in Germany this training takes much longer. He also considered that the quality of a French doctorate did not correspond to an American PhD.

EUROPEAN AND US BIOTECHNOLOGY APPLICATIONS

There were several common themes in companies' answers about how they use biotechnology, and a variation in such applications between Europe and the US. Both the European and US laboratories apply biotechnology as a set of research tools and techniques to pharmaceutical research. These techniques can help improve understanding of the origin and development of disease and assist better identification of targets for conventional drugs. The majority of pharmaceuticals companies also told us that biotechnology is now part of the entire discovery process, from basic research right through to clinical trials.

In seeds, biotechnology supplies basic underpinning research. In agrochemicals, biotechnology techniques are used to help identify targets for plant protection products. Two of the three companies we interviewed in this area carried out the majority of their molecular biology research in Europe, with field trials taking place abroad close to their major markets.

A second common theme to emerge in pharmaceuticals and diagnostics was that much of the work in US laboratories is concerned with the clinical development processes required to get US Food and Drug Administration (FDA) approval for products and with taking products to market. World regulatory standards are set by the FDA, and companies which pass US regulatory hurdles and clinical trials gain world-wide acceptance for their products. Thus US laboratories are often used to develop compounds which emerge from research anywhere in the world and to carry out clinical trials according to FDA regulations. Alternatively, clinical development is carried out in countries where clinical research standards are acceptable to the FDA. One company told us that its clinical trials are conducted only to the standards of the FDA, but that development sometimes has to take place in parallel in the US and Europe for regulatory reasons. Another company duplicates some European efforts in the US, because FDA development requirements in infectious diseases are stricter than elsewhere. A third company focuses its regulatory efforts on the FDA. Once FDA approval has been gained, the results are sent to other countries which may 'tweak' these or do whatever local trials are necessary to meet local needs.

Several companies mentioned the significant advantages that had accrued to them from having a long-term relationship with the FDA regarding approval of manufacturing plant for second-generation biotechnology products (plasma products, vaccines, and so on). It was relatively easy for them to have facilities approved for biotechnology products. For companies which lack such facilities, there are complicated regulatory issues concerning manufacturing approvals for recombinant proteins, especially if manufacturing is out-sourced from a DBF. Although the majority of companies are using biotechnology to develop a range of in-vitro pre-clinical tests, for instance toxicology or safety tests, the FDA was considered a barrier to these tests replacing in-vivo tests. The FDA is not ready to accept surrogate markers and still wants drugs to be tested in people.

No clear pattern emerged for the location of development efforts targeted towards biotechnology products or processes. One company had no biotechnology products and none in the pipeline. A few companies carried out development in Europe only and one company was involved in development at the US site only. The majority, however, are using biotechnology for product and process development in both locations.

Seven companies have decided to invest in gene therapy and five in genomics, and these activities usually involve collaborations, investments or acquisitions of external partners. Before discussing these external collaborations in more detail, it is relevant to mention the response of two companies to the restrictive German genetic laws passed in the mid 1980s.

These genetic laws were implemented locally by the *Länder* and involved discretionary decisions based on local political views about genetic engineering. The first company carries out its biotechnology research only in Germany, and also manufactures therapeutic proteins there. It has never found the regulatory environment a problem, but its plant is located in a pro-industry *Länd* which appears to have implemented gene law in a loose fashion. The second company was just about to build a production plant for protein therapeutics in Germany at the time the gene law was passed. The local *Länd* did not give approval for this facility. This led to it setting up US research and production facilities.[2] Although German gene law has now been amended and there is no longer a barrier to German production, the availability of spare capacity in the US rules out that possibility in the short term.

EXTERNAL RESEARCH

All the companies are involved in collaborations with university or public sector research (PSR) and with new biotechnology firms (DBFs) to build up in-house competences. Some links with PSR have been crucial to companies' initial competence building in biotechnology, and several companies have current large collaborations designed to bring genomics and gene therapy knowledge in-house. It was difficult to get a clear picture of the proportion of in-house R&D budgets being spent on external collaborations in biotechnology. Some companies either could not or would not provide this information. Some companies control external R&D expenditure tightly and are aware of the proportion involved; others delegate it to individual laboratories or make investments in strategic collaborations on a case-by-case basis, allocating additional funds from corporate budgets as necessary. The spend on external alliances is also complicated in companies which have a corporate investment division. Given these limitations, Table 7.3, which is based both on our interviews and on press reports, sets out a rough indication of the percentage of total R&D expenditure allocated to external biotechnology research.

As is indicated by company J, strategic alliances are generally more expensive than university collaborations, and may be funded from general corporate budgets rather than from R&D budgets. For instance, one US laboratory spends 1 per cent of its research budget on university research but the European HQ[3] has topped up the total US research budget by 15 per cent to finance one DBF alliance. The larger-scale expenditure on strategic alliances than on university collaborations reflects the fact that companies anticipate getting much more out of the former, for example appropriating

Table 7.3 Cost of external research as a proportion of total R&D

Company

A 3% on university research. Additional allocations for strategic alliances
B 10% – sometimes more
C Over 10%
D 5% on university research. Additional allocations for strategic alliances
E Over 5%
F 3–5% with plans to increase to 10%
G 3% on university research. Additional allocations for strategic alliances
H Very low. University links to be increased
I 10% on university links and strategic alliances. Additional funds for equity investments in DBFs
J 4% on university research and 15% for strategic alliances

---

technologies which they wish to bring in-house. Alliances with DBFs enable firms to move quickly into new areas of research and gain critical expertise. PSR is slower to produce things of immediate relevance, but it is important in searching for new ideas, techniques, for specific pieces of contract research and for recruitment. The main advantage of external links is that they provide a lot of flexibility in getting in and out of activities and in sharing the risk with someone else.

In addition to collaborations with university research and DBFs, six of the ten companies are involved in research collaborations (or joint ventures) with other medium to large-sized companies; some partners are in the same sector and others are potential users of the technology being developed. At least ten collaborations with partners from the US, Europe and Japan were mentioned, and were in pharmaceuticals, diagnostics and seeds. These collaborations were thought to be a growing trend.

Collaborations with University Research

All the companies fund university research but only half of them second staff to the university laboratories where they place research contracts. The majority of European laboratories have many more collaborations with European than with US PSR, and tend to have arrangements with universities in the same country as their HQ. French companies, for instance, collaborate with the Centre National de la Recherche Scientifique or Institut Pasteur, German companies with Max Planck Institutes and British companies with British universities. One UK company commented that it had tried to link with Max Planck Institutes in Germany and the Institut National de la Recherche Acronomique in France, but had been given the impression that these public research organizations were not prepared to do a deal with a foreign company; they saw it as their duty to give first preference to national firms. Only one company mentioned Framework programmes as a means to build links with PSR around Europe; this company had recently submitted its first proposal to the EU.

Two European laboratories had no US university links at all, but there is one whose only academic collaboration is in the US, and this is a very large, long-term commitment. Another European laboratory said that an increasing proportion of its university links are in the US. In order to find the best academic partners in one specific area, it had recently set up a formal process to select the best academic people in European and North American universities. This had led to collaboration with a US university, selected from a short-list which was composed predominantly of North American universities. We were reminded that collaborations with US academics may differ from their European counterparts, since many of those in US PSR with industrial contracts are trying to turn themselves into DBFs. The majority of the US laboratories' PSR collaborations are local to the US, and four laboratories have links only with US PSR. The small number of collaborations with European PSR are usually in the same country as corporate HQ.

Strategic Alliances with DBFs

The companies involved in the study had a range of different arrangements for linking up with DBFs, ranging from acquisitions to investments, strategic alliances and licensing. The majority of strategic alliances are in the health area. Companies mentioned a small number of current agreements with US DBFs in the seeds/plant protection area, but are of the opinion that these will decrease in the future, because the number of independent companies in plant biotechnology is shrinking.

The European sites of the companies are involved in 20–30 significant strategic alliances with US DBFs, including some very large investments and some acquisitions. These expensive arrangements in the US tend to be funded from European HQ, with the US laboratories acting as licensing agents/talent spotters. Some companies are currently increasing their portfolios of strategic alliances in the US; others have terminated such arrangements or are cutting back on the scale of their arrangements.

Strategic alliances between European companies and European DBFs are rare; those which exist are mainly with UK and French DBFs. The

US laboratories appear to be less involved in strategic alliances than their European counterparts; those that exist are mainly with North American DBFs.

The majority of knowledge flowing through these strategic alliances is from the US DBF to the European laboratories. Though one or two companies are trying to encourage their US laboratories to make direct contact with US DBF partners where this might be relevant, the main way for the US laboratories to acquire knowledge generated through the European laboratories' strategic alliances is through a company's formal international research committee meetings.

TECHNOLOGY TRANSFER BETWEEN LABORATORIES

Few companies have yet developed satisfactory methods for diffusing knowledge developed in one laboratory to company scientists in other locations. Some have not even thought about intra-company technology transfer. Every company organizes regular meetings of senior research directors from their various laboratories. These meetings are used to discuss a wide variety of issues such as research programmes, strategy, regulation and alliances with DBFs, and to present research reports. Research directors, in theory, are the means by which knowledge about what is happening in various laboratories permeates down to appropriate research groups. Companies also have systems for exchanging research reports; in the best examples all types of report – on exploratory ideas, progress reports and final reports – are widely available to all levels of staff throughout the company. Other companies exchange reports infrequently and restrict circulation to libraries and specific individuals such as research directors. One US laboratory complained that it was not sent research reports of European collaborations, a problem compounded because these reports are not written in English. Most companies hold corporate scientific meetings, but often these are not company-wide or lack bench scientist involvement. Short-term exchanges of staff between laboratories – for a few weeks – are quite common. Staff usually go to another company laboratory to learn new techniques or to train colleagues. Only six companies had arrangements for longer-term placements abroad, and this happened rather infrequently. The aim of these long-term placements abroad is to support the career development of outstanding young scientists. The general experience is that these scientists return to Europe at the end of their placements.

We found little evidence to suggest that the use of information and communications technology (ICT) is facilitating international communication between laboratories. Four companies use e-mail and three companies teleconference. One company reported that US–European e-mail interaction (at a senior level) is easier than intra-company e-mail in Europe, because so few European staff have been placed on the Internet. Another company, which has recently introduced e-mail internationally, has found that this facility is underused by bench scientists; the lack of personal contacts at other sites is a barrier to interaction. Teleconferencing is used to replace some face-to-face meetings by high level managers and one company uses it for presenting research results. Teleconferencing saves the time and cost involved in transporting people around the world, but companies have not yet worked out the best way to exploit the new facility. Problems are caused by gaps between talking and hearing, not being able to jump into a conversation to make a point and the lack of eye contact around the table. Although it does have its uses, it is thought unlikely ever to substitute fully for face-to-face meetings.

This section ends with a report on the company which seems furthest down the road in terms of building mechanisms to encourage knowledge flow between its UK and US laboratories. The company recognizes the importance of integrating the work of these laboratories, and the organization of research on a matrix system is a means to this end.[4] It is trying to encourage links between the US and European laboratories, with each other's partners and vice versa. In addition to frequent meetings between senior R&D staff at the two sites, a variety of other mechanisms is employed. There has been a major investment in electronically networking the entire company, from top management to bench scientists. They have round-the-clock computer communication throughout the company and use highly advanced computer technology to encourage frequent transatlantic communication. Every US scientist is computer linked to every European scientist. There is also a company rule that any time any US scientist travels to Europe (or a European scientist travels to the US) – for a conference, for example – they have to spend two to three additional days at the sister laboratory, in order to get to know their colleagues and the work they are doing. This personal interaction can form the basis for facilitating e-mail communication between laboratories. There are also several other methods for exchanging research results between laboratories:

1. *A research database (access to which is determined by seniority)*. Every research programme is reviewed annually and review documents are placed in the database. The database also contains summaries of all research programmes and quarterly up-dates on progress.

2. *A variety of scientific company meetings.* Company scientists publish a lot and attend and speak at general scientific conferences. Every department runs a seminar programme where people from other parts of the company and external speakers are invited to speak about their research.
3. *There are many short-term exchanges of scientists.* Staff at every level, including technicians, go on short-term exchanges to the sister laboratory. These exchanges last anywhere from two to three weeks up to several months. Some people have had longer periods of work in each other's environments. When they return, they give talks about what they have learned at the other site and the research carried out there.

Despite all these efforts, distance and the differing cultures at the two laboratories remain major barriers to the intra-company flow of knowledge. The company thinks it very important, however, to retain some element of cultural identity in the two laboratories. They operate differently, but the cultural tensions which result are very creative.

COMPARISON OF US AND EUROPEAN RESEARCH ENVIRONMENTS

PSR

Those interviewed all agree that the main characteristic which distinguishes US from European PSR is its scale. The US biotechnology science base is described as having 'ten times more universities than Europe', 'more science' and 'critical mass because of the sheer numbers involved'; it is 'strong and dominant', 'very progressive and innovative' and 'avid for novelty'. Within the US, Boston is identified as having the world's largest concentration of biotechnology research, which makes it possible to find an expert in almost any specialty. The greater pool of scientific talent provides companies with choice because, 'in any scientific area there will be three or four laboratories, with good top "young lions" as well as key investigators. You can select the people you want to work with rather than being stuck with a single option'.

High levels of US funding for PSR also result in very good laboratories, equipment and research, which attract the world's best scientists, including many European professors and post-doctoral researchers. Moreover, the number of laboratories in the US allows them to negotiate better prices from vendors of scientific equipment. For example, one US laboratory paid 40 per cent less than the French HQ for a piece of equipment bought from a European company.

There are also problems. The ready availability of US research funds is thought to make it more difficult for companies to direct the work of top academic researchers into new areas. The ease with which top researchers can secure public funds to pursue their own ideas makes them very independent. Collaborations with US universities are thought to be more expensive than in the UK.

Molecular biology has also diffused more rapidly into general training in the US than in the UK. For instance, in the US, molecular biology is now part of courses for pharmacologists, pathologists and medical consultants, and there are good educational programmes in areas unknown to UK universities, for example molecular pathology and molecular neurology. One of those interviewed told us that:

> US medical registration authorities have changed the rules of what they expect a consultant doctor to do. Top class consultants in the US work in molecular biology labs, but that is unheard of in the UK where consultants are still trained in time-honoured fashion, with surgical experience, but the idea that consultants should do molecular biology research is unheard of.

Very few people had any overview of European PSR in biotechnology. One British research director had wide knowledge of European science; he thought French PSR was the best in Europe, closely followed by the UK and Germany. Spain was improving fast, and thought capable of overtaking Italy, but that still left these two countries far behind the leaders. By contrast, although French companies considered French PSR to be of high quality, they criticized its lack of critical mass and the institutional inertia which affected its capacity to focus on strategic areas, particularly in plant biotechnology. Apart from a few areas such as nitrogen fixation and male sterility, French PSR was characterized as a 'good follower'.

The majority of people, however, were generally aware only of the science base in the country of company HQ, reflecting the fact that European PSR is very fragmented and not viewed as a single entity in the same way as US PSR. The quality of science in France, Britain and Germany is considered to be comparable with that in the US; the main difference is the lower quantity. A few think that European science is more solid and systematic than in the US and more creative. However, European academic scientists differ from their American counterparts in lacking an understanding of industry and its perspective and in being poor at translating their work into products. Specific concerns were expressed about the UK as an academic environment. Research training is capital intensive, but academic research is under-capitalized and that has affected academic research in the biotechnology area:

There are still some centres of excellence, like Cambridge and Oxford. But outside those centres of excellence, the UK has been in relative decline in terms of the physical and equipment infrastructure and all the modern machines, which has implications for the training of the next generation of scientists to do research. The UK was a world leader in sequencing technology, but it has lost that lead.

European competence is highly praised in plant biotechnology, molecular biology, structural sequencing and in the human genome programme; there are perceived to be gaps in microbial and mammalian areas and in combinatorial chemistry. Another major concern is that European biotechnology training is concentrated in areas such as cell biology, molecular biology and immunology, while there is a need for greater breadth. There were also anxieties about wider trends in biotechnology research in pharmaceuticals, with implications for both US and European policy. In the words of one of those interviewed:

> Such a heavy emphasis in biotechnology has been put on identifying initial targets that downstream efforts may have difficulty in finding relevant compounds. There has been so much focus on molecular biology that clinical pharmacology and chemistry capabilities have been neglected. There are not enough good people out there in these fields. Combinatorial chemistry will drive up the need for chemists and good pharmacologists will become more important. But there is too much focus and concern on the front end of all this. Perhaps there will be some re-emphasis in relation to antibiotics. It is very much needed in relation to antibiotics. The last new antibiotic class discovered was in 1976 and antibiotic-resistant bacteria are on the rise, but nobody understands microbial pathology or does research in that area anymore

DBFs

The higher number of DBFs in the US than Europe is explained by the general environment. The US in general is just more risk accepting and interested in novelty. Academics are very entrepreneurial and well supported by venture capital, which makes it easy for scientists to get investments for their companies. Moreover, scientists regard working in DBFs as an attractive career option. US DBFs are thought to be especially good in genomics and gene therapy; European DBFs are not thought to offer expertise in these two areas, although some praised genomics work in France, Germany and the UK. Overall, US DBFs are considered less strong in agricultural than pharmaceutical applications. One European company had originally found it unavoidable to link with US DBFs in plant biotechnology; now it gets relevant knowledge from national PSR.

By contrast, the DBF sector in Europe is considered small and underdeveloped. The main problems are lack of venture capital and poor capability (or interest) of academics in commercializing their work. Those with knowledge of UK DBFs consider them to be 'real businesses doing science', whilst a lot of US DBFs are venture capital investment vehicles only, which are trying to raise money to finance their operations.

Other

There is a consensus among all those interviewed that the US is a far more favourable climate for commercializing biotechnology than Europe. There is more public acceptance of biotechnology in the US and people seem readier to accept the use of genetic manipulation; Europeans are too prone to enter into moral debates about such uses, creating a difficult environment for gene therapy approaches. One of those interviewed identified Northern European countries with an Anglo-Saxon culture as having a particularly hostile attitude towards biotechnology. Green Party activities are thought to be largely responsible for this anti-science climate.

The US also benefits from having a very pro-industry policy environment, with the government providing tax credits for companies which carry out R&D and Congress exerting great pressure for FDA regulations to be softened. We were also told that Europe lacked a tradition of picking up families of people with genetic disorders and working with them, as is possible in the US. The UK National Health Service (NHS) used to track family histories in genetic disorders, providing a background resource to support gene disorder research. The break-up of the NHS means that this resource no longer exists, making it difficult to carry out population pedigree analysis. Such analyses have been commercialized in the US.

A very large number of those interviewed, however, identified regulation and patenting as the most significant differences affecting commercialization in the two regions. In comparison with the US, Europe's lack of a defined system for risk assessment of environmental release has created a difficult environment for biotechnology in agriculture and food. The US also has a better regulatory environment for the genetic manipulation of organisms in the laboratory. Regulation in the US is regarded as very professional and tight but much less restrictive than in Europe. In Europe, for instance, some types of biotechnology research require a P3 laboratory; the US might require only a P1 or P2.

In comparing regulation in various European countries, British companies described the UK as recognizing the balance which is needed between risk assessment and management in the laboratory, and the competitive development of products. The UK had taken an active role in trying to influence the EU regulatory environment by pressing for a legal framework which is product rather than process oriented. This view is reported in the House of Lords (1993) report on the regulation of genetically modified organisms. It considers that the balance of risk and benefit should be driven by the risks in the final product rather than any risks inherent in some of the processes leading up to the product. Europe seems to be driven more by the latter (process oriented) view. The former would lead to a less restrictive environment for regulating biotechnology and would be closer to what is the norm in the US. If the latter view becomes the basis for European regulation, it could lead to more biotechnology being undertaken in the US. Another regulatory problem is the delay and lack of transparency in European Commission procedures for approving products. In building up applications for product approval, companies found it almost impossible to foresee what would cause delays.

In terms of clinical trials for diagnostic products, however, we were told that some countries in Europe have a much easier regulatory system than the US (especially related to HIV). In the US some diagnostic products require two years of clinical trials followed by two years for regulatory approval; following successful clinical trials in Europe, the same product may take six months only for regulatory approval. For some products clinical trials in Europe take only one month. Therefore, it is usual for biotechnology firms to launch diagnostics products in Europe[5] before the US.

In Europe, regulatory efforts by the EC are seen to support harmonization, and those responsible in the Commission are regarded as being well disposed to the development of biotechnology, unlike the European Parliament. Failure of the European Parliament to approve the EC's directive on patenting in 1995 was expected to lead to intense pressure for a new directive.

CONCLUSIONS

This study focused on five major questions about companies' European and US research activities: the relative numbers of biotechnology researchers in each region; the nature of biotechnology R&D employed; methods for acquiring and transferring biotechnology capabilities in and between home and overseas laboratories; the factors influencing the location of company biotechnology research in the US; and the effect of overseas research on European biotechnology capabilities.

Companies employ roughly twice as many biotechnology researchers in Europe as in their US laboratories, but the US laboratories often recruit European-born researchers from among post-doctorates at leading US universities. European researchers seconded to the US laboratories are few in number and normally return home at the end of their placements. There is no great difference in the type of biotechnology research carried out in Europe and the US in pharmaceuticals, except for the emphasis on clinical development in the US demanded by FDA regulations. In agricultural biotechnology, however, the majority of molecular biology research is carried out in Europe, with the US mainly involved in field trials and plant breeding.

Companies build in-house competences through external collaborations with PSR and strategic alliances with DBFs. Most university alliances are local to each laboratory. The majority of strategic alliances are with US-based DBFs and are controlled by European corporate HQ; most are in pharmaceuticals and involve knowledge flowing from the US DBF to the European HQ. The major reasons for the location of laboratories in the US are the size of the market, the need to comply with FDA regulations and the desire to tap into US science. However, companies have found that the general environment for commercializing biotechnology is more friendly in the US than Europe, especially in terms of regulation and patenting but also general public acceptance for biotechnology.

The results of the study indicate that the US activities of European chemical/pharmaceutical multinationals, particularly their links with DBFs, are helping to increase their biotechnology capabilities in Europe in areas where Europe has weaknesses, for instance in gene therapy, genomics and combinatorial chemistry. In some areas where European PSR is weak, such as microbial physiology and virology, the shift of corporate activities to the US is exacerbating existing weaknesses.

The study also produced other findings which have implications for multinational corporate strategy and for European science, training and regulatory policy. Companies have not yet adequately addressed the problem of how to diffuse and integrate the scientific and technological knowledge being accumulated in globally dispersed R&D laboratories. We found little evidence to suggest that ICT will support such knowledge flow. The few companies experimenting with ICT found it useful, but not a complete replacement for face-to-face contact.

In relation to EU policy we found, first, that in comparison with the US, Europe's science base lacks critical mass due to its fragmented and somewhat chauvinistic character. National PSR, for its part, appears to be more supportive of national than other European companies. Companies, for their part, appear to have little knowledge of overall European PSR expertise in biotechnology. In part this may reflect the historic focus of Framework programmes in biotechnology on basic, academic research rather than on strategic research involving collaborations with industry. This focus has given little opportunity for companies to build relationships with PSR competence around the EU as it has in other technologies. Support for university–industry links in biotechnology in the UK has been an important method for companies to explore university expertise in biotechnology (Senker and Sharp, 1988). Recent EU attempts to increase industrial involvement in its biotechnology programmes may remedy this problem, especially if programmes promote intra-Community university/ industry research collaborations.

Companies are moving some areas of research to the US because of gaps in European expertise – namely in microbial and mammalian areas, bio-informatics and combinatorial chemistry. Companies expressed concern about the lack of breadth in European research, with over-concentration on cell biology, molecular biology and immunology. Europe also lacks a background resource to support gene disorder research. The US, however, shares Europe's weakness in failing to direct research towards the discovery of new classes of antibiotic.

Second, our results indicate possible deficiencies in European research and training which need to be addressed. The main loss of talent from Europe to the US is at post-doctoral level. We do not know whether scientists are attracted to work in the US by the science or whether limited opportunities and conditions for post-doctoral work in Europe drive them abroad. For instance, we were told that academic biotechnology research in Europe is adversely affected by under-capitalization and that European PSR is less well equipped than that in the US. Post-doctoral training abroad is advantageous to all concerned, but there may be cause for concern if a large proportion of European post-doctoral researchers are subsequently recruited to work in the US. These findings suggest that the opportunities and conditions for post-doctoral research in Europe should be reviewed.

Moreover, it appears that in the UK, and perhaps in other European countries, molecular biology is not diffusing into general medical training in a way which supports the commercialization of biotechnology. There may be a need to modernize training for pharmacologists, pathologists and medical consultants, incorporating new courses such as molecular pathology and neurology.

Finally, we found that FDA regulations are a significant influence on the establishment of R&D laboratories in the US. It is not clear how acceptable FDA regulations would be to member states which have more or less stringent requirements, but this problem has not yet been solved by EU directives. The duplication of clinical trials in Europe and the US appears unnecessarily expensive and time consuming. While not minimizing the political difficulties involved, it would appear beneficial for negotiations between the FDA and EU regulatory authorities to attempt to harmonize regulations and begin to work out the basis upon which mutual recognition of clinical trials might be achieved.

The results of the study indicate that leading-edge biotechnology R&D by multinationals is not leaving Europe for the US, and thus not affecting European research capabilities. The study is reassuring in indicating that Europe is maintaining its capabilities in the mainstream areas of biotechnology. However, US out-sourcing of R&D in specialist areas suggests that, if it is to retain its position, Europe needs to nurture centres of expertise in areas such as combinatorial chemistry and bio-informatics.

NOTES

1. The study was funded by the BIOTECH Programme of the European Commission, DG XII. The Science, Technology, Energy and Environment Research Programme (STEEP) at SPRU, funded by the ESRC, also made a contribution towards the costs. We are grateful to Margaret Sharp of SPRU, University of Sussex and Emmanuel Weisenburger of BETA, Université Louis Pasteur, Strasbourg, for their assistance with this study.
2. Some people think that the US operation was developed because biotechnology production was not allowed in Germany. A group of senior researchers used the rejection as a means of mobilizing top management support for the US facility (interview information).
3. In the interests of clarity, all European sites are referred to as 'HQ', although this is not always a true representation of the status of the companies.
4. Research is organized by disease areas; there are also departments responsible for various disciplines (for example, biotechnology, cell biology) and methods for relevant skills to diffuse into every research group as needed.
5. Particularly in France and Spain. Italy and Germany are beginning to be more difficult and the UK has never been an easy environment (interview information).

REFERENCES

House of Lords Select Committee on Science and Technology (1993), *Regulation of the United Kingdom Biotechnology Industry and Global Competitiveness*, HL Papers 80-I and 80-II, London: HMSO.

Senker, J. and M. Sharp (1988), *The Biotechnology Directorate of the SERC. Report and Evaluation of its Achievements – 1981–87*, Report to the Management Committee of the Biotechnology Directorate, Brighton: Science Policy Research Unit, University of Sussex.

Senker, J., P. -B. Joly and M. Reinhard (1996), *Overseas Biotechnology Research by Europe's Chemical/Pharmaceuticals Multinationals: Rationale and Implications*, STEEP Discussion Paper No. 33, Brighton: Science Policy Research Unit, University of Sussex.

Sharp, M., S. Thomas and P. Martin (1993), *Technology Transfer and Innovation Policy: Chemicals and Biotechnology*, STEEP Discussion Paper No. 6, Brighton: Science Policy Research Unit, University of Sussex.

8. The 'commercialization gap' in gene therapy: lessons for European competitiveness

Paul Martin and Sandy Thomas

INTRODUCTION

Somatic gene therapy promises to be one of the most important developments in medicine during the next few decades.[1] It is a radical new technology which uses DNA as a therapeutic agent either to correct the genetic defects which cause a particular illness or to help restore normal functions to diseased cells. The first clinical trials have indicated that gene therapy techniques might be successfully used to treat not only genetic diseases, such as cystic fibrosis, but also some of the most important and intractable non-genetic diseases, ranging from AIDS to cancer. As a consequence analysts are predicting a billion dollar market for gene therapy products in the next five years.

Most gene therapy research is taking place in the US. Already over 160 clinical trials are underway or planned to start, and some 20 dedicated gene therapy companies have been founded with a combined market value of over $1 billion. The US has also led the world in establishing an ethical and regulatory framework for the introduction of gene therapy. In contrast, Europe is significantly behind the US. About 46 clinical trials have been initiated, several governments are establishing ethical and regulatory frameworks, and ten European dedicated gene therapy companies have been founded.

This chapter is based on a project funded by the BIOTECH Programme of the European Commission, DG XII[2] which sought to examine the development of gene therapy and assess both its potential socio-economic impacts and Europe's competitiveness in this area. In particular it will focus on one of the key findings of the study, namely the apparent 'commercialization gap' leading to the under-exploitation of the technology in Europe, and suggest ways in which this might be overcome.

The Long-Term Impact of Gene Therapy on Medicine and the Pharmaceutical Industry

The prospects for the development of gene therapy in the next ten years have been greatly overstated, and will be limited to a few diseases such as cancer, cystic fibrosis and HIV/AIDS. However, in the longer term there are good reasons for believing that it will become a key medical technology. In particular, it is a misapprehension to think of gene therapy as one technology. Instead it is more useful to conceive of gene transfer techniques as a broad set of enabling technologies.[3] These methods are already being successfully applied to almost every tissue or organ in model systems and are under investigation for a very wide range of human diseases (see Table 8.1). In principle, gene transfer could be used to treat almost any part of the body. Therapeutic interventions using gene transfer will, moreover, become increasingly feasible as definitive information accumulates about the human genome, leading to the identification of genes involved in common diseases and a better understanding of the molecular processes of pathology. Gene therapy also presents a number of potential advantages over the use of conventional drug therapies, in that the therapeutic can be targeted and its mode of action better characterized.[4] As a consequence, gene therapy has the potential to create a new class of therapeutics which could have a major impact on medicine in the 21st century.

In the 1980s gene therapy was seen largely as an *ex-vivo* procedure[5] for genetic diseases, and it was anticipated that it would be commercially developed within a separate industrial sector from the biopharmaceutical industry. This was true until the early 1990s, with all the key developments in the field occurring in small, dedicated gene therapy firms. Increasingly, however, gene therapy is being conceived of in terms of a novel form of drug therapy for many commonly acquired diseases and is seen as a source of new therapeutic products for the pharmaceutical industry (Martin, 1995). The majority of the gene therapy products currently under development can, moreover, fit easily into existing pharmaceutical markets and distribution chains. As a consequence, gene therapy firms are being rapidly integrated into the pharmaceutical industry, through acquisitions and research alliances, to provide new drug products for large firms. Earlier predictions of gene therapy posing a major threat to existing pharmaceutical companies now appear unfounded as the emergence of a separate industrial sector is unlikely.

To some extent the incorporation of gene therapy into the pharmaceutical industry is part of a broader shift to biological rather than small molecule therapies, driven by the emergence of genomics and the further

Table 8.1 Disease targets for gene therapy

Genetic disease	Cancer	Cardiovascular disease	Viral disease	Neurological disorders	Other chronic conditions	Other conditions
ADA/SCID[1]	Leukaemia	Atherosclerosis	HIV	Parkinson's	Arthritis	Wound healing/burns
Gaucher's	Breast	Peripheral vascular	Hepatitis	Alzheimer's	Diabetes	Kidney disease
Lesch-Nyhan	Ovarian	disease	CMV[2]		Liver diseases	Dental problems
Cystic fibrosis	Melanoma	Restenosis			Emphysema	Eye disease
Duchenne Muscular	Lung				Skin ulcers	Skin disease
Dystrophy	Renal					Baldness
Familial	Glioma					
hyper-cholesterolemia						
Thallassaemia						
Haemophilia						

Notes:
1. Adenosine Deaminase / Severe Combined Immune Deficiency.
2. Cytomegalovirus.

132

development of protein therapeutics. At present many pharmaceutical companies are still cautious about the prospects for gene therapy, but investment is being made on an increasing scale and at a more rapid pace. There are strong reasons therefore for believing that, in the medium term, gene therapy will have a major impact on both the types of therapy developed and the innovative activities of the pharmaceutical industry. It is therefore vital that Europe has a strong scientific and commercial presence in this area.

Analysing the 'Gene Therapy Innovation System'

Given the long-term potential of gene therapy, a central question for the research study was to assess European industrial competitiveness in this key area compared with the US, and to explain any relative weakness. The study comprised a general overview of gene therapy in Europe and a detailed case study of a leading European Union (EU) member state, the UK, for comparison with the US.

In order to enable a systematic comparison, a simplified 'map' of what might be called the 'gene therapy innovation system' was used (see Figure 8.1). The innovation system described shows the principal groups involved in creating this new technology (scientists, clinicians, gene therapy firms and regulators) and the relationships between them. The activities of each of these groups and their interactions were examined in the UK and compared with the US, and any national differences in the organization of the system or these interactions were analysed.

The main groups shown in Figure 8.1 include scientists in public research institutions, hospital-based clinicians, agencies involved in the regulation of research and the control of new medicinal products, large pharmaceutical companies, dedicated gene therapy firms and the venture capitalists involved in their creation. At the centre of the map of the innovation system is the testing of gene therapies through the process of clinical trials. If a new therapy can be successfully taken through a series of clinical trials to demonstrate both efficacy and safety, then it can be launched as a new product on the market. The idea of an innovation system is purely heuristic, but is useful in allowing a more systematic analysis of the key elements and the dynamic processes linking them. In particular, it helps enable a detailed comparison between the development of gene therapy in the US and the UK.

The chapter is organized in three sections. The first gives a brief overview of gene therapy in Europe compared with the US, the second describes the case study comparison between the innovation systems in the UK and the US, and conclusions will be given in the third part.

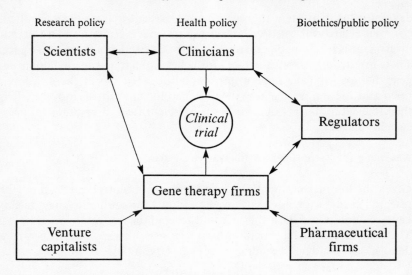

Figure 8.1 *The gene therapy innovation system*

THE DEVELOPMENT OF GENE THERAPY IN EUROPE AND THE US

In general, Europe lags significantly behind the US in the development of gene therapy. This can be shown by comparing a number of indicators covering basic research, clinical development and the commercialization of the technology.

Basic Research

The Science Citation Index (SCI) shows that US researchers published nearly twice as many gene therapy-related papers (60 per cent of total) compared with European authors (30 per cent of total) between 1981 and 1993 (see Figure 8.2). This reflects both the dominant position of US biomedical research in general and the leading role American researchers have played in the emergence of gene therapy. However, the European proportion of publications is roughly what would be expected from its overall share of all biomedical papers[6] and there is some evidence to suggest that the US lead is being eroded (Martin and Thomas, 1996, p. 19).

Clinical Development

Comparing the number of clinical trials of gene therapy, there are about three times as many in the US as in Europe. As of June 1996, 161 gene therapy trials had been approved to start in the US, while only 46 trials had commenced in Europe. European trials are generally at an earlier stage, the first trial having started three years after the initial US trial. However, the overall pattern of therapeutic strategies and disease targets is similar in Europe and the US.

Dedicated Gene Therapy Firms

In the US there are 16 dedicated gene therapy firms, six cell therapy firms working on gene therapy, and four other biopharmaceutical companies sponsoring gene therapy clinical trials.[7] In contrast, there are nine dedicated gene therapy firms in Europe, one cell therapy firm working on gene therapy, and no biopharmaceutical companies sponsoring clinical trials (see Tables 8.2, 8.3 and 8.4). Dedicated European gene therapy firms are not only younger, having been founded three to five years after their US counterparts, but are smaller, employing a total of 300 staff compared with 900 staff in US gene therapy companies.

However, it should be noted that these figures probably overstate the strength of the European gene therapy industry for two reasons. First, one European firm, Transgene, accounts for over half the total number of staff employed by the industry and only three of the ten companies were involved in sponsoring trials. Second, there are a much larger number of general biopharmaceutical companies in the US working on gene therapy (32) compared with Europe (4), with some of these making significant investments in this area.[8]

SCI publications containing the term 'gene therapy', 1981–93

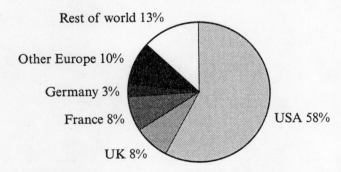

Figure 8.2 Breakdown of gene therapy publications by country

Table 8.2   The US gene therapy industry: dedicated gene therapy firms (December 1996)

Public	Date Founded	No. of Staff[1]	Private	Date Founded	No. of Staff
Avigen	1992	35	Canji[5]	1990	55
GeneMedicine	1992	70	Genetix	1992	2
Genetic Therapy[2]	1987	150	Genovo	1992	not known
Somatix[3]	1988	110	GenVec	1993	35
Targeted Genetics	1989	65	Ingenex	1993	16
TKT	1988	65	Introgen	1993	40
Viagene[4]	1987	140	Megabios	1992	35
Vical	1987	85	RGene[6]	1994	8
Total		720			175

Notes:
1. Scientists and technicians.
2. Acquired by Sandoz in 1995.
3. Acquired by Cell Genesys in 1997.
4. Acquired by Chiron in 1995.
5. Acquired by Schering Plough in 1996.
6. Acquired by Targeted Genetics in 1996.

Table 8.3(a)   The US gene therapy industry: cell therapy firms (December 1996)

Public	Date Founded	No. of Staff[1]	Private	Date Founded	No. of Staff
AIS[1]	1982	150	Aastrom	1989	45
Cell Genesys	1988	135	Amcell	not known	not known
Cellcor	1986	43	Activated Cell Therapy	not known	not known
CellPro	1987	180	Cell Therapeutics	1995	22
Cytotherapeutics	1988	100	Genzyme Tissue Repair	not known	not known
Systemix[2]	1988	200	Neocrin	1992	38
			Progenitor	1992	38
Total		808	Total		139

Notes:
1. Acquired by Rhone-Poulenc Rorer in 1995.
2. Acquired by Sandoz in 1996.

Table 8.3(b) The US gene therapy industry: biotechnology firms working on gene therapy (December 1996)

	Year founded	No. of staff		Year founded	No. of staff
Advanced Therapies	1993	not known	Enzo	1976	280
Agracetus	1981	107	Epoch	not known	not known
Alexion Pharmaceuticals	1992	48	Genetronics	1983	not known
Alkermes	1987	108			
Anticancer Inc.	1984	20	Genzyme	1981	2000
Apollon	1992	39	Geron	1990	not known
Ariad	1991	85			
Atlantic Pharmaceuticals	not known	not known	Gliatech	1988	37
			Immunicon	1984	30
Aviron	1992	55	Ixion Biotech	1993	5
BioStratum	not known	not known	Oncorpharm	1994	14
			Onyx Pharmaceuticals	1992	55
Biotransplant	1990	48	PharmaGenics	1990	40
Boron Biologics	1986	17	Repligen	1981	290
Centocor	1979	550	Therion Biologics	1991	34
Cephalon	1987	175	Transcell Technologies	1991	30
Chiron	1981	2600	Virus Research Institute	1991	44
CV Therapeutics	1992	65			
Cytrx	1985	40			

Table 8.4(a) The European gene therapy industry (December 1996)

Dedicated Firms		Date Founded	No. of staff
Bavarian Nordic	Den	1994	9
Cell Genix	Ger	1994	20
Genopoietic	Fra	not known	not known
HepaVec	Ger	1995	5
IntroGene	Neth	1993	17
MediGene	Ger	1994	25
Orthogen	Ger	1992	not known
Oxford BioMedica	UK	1996	5
Therexsys	UK	1992	30
Transgene	Fra	1980	180
Total			290

Table 8.4(b)   European biotechnology firms working on gene therapy

Cantab Pharmaceuticals (UK)
Celltech (UK)
Genzyme (UK)
IDM (Fra)

Pharmaceutical Companies' Investment in Gene Therapy

One indicator of the pharmaceutical industry's investment in this technology is the number of alliances and acquisitions by large firms, and the
total value of these investments. Interestingly, European pharmaceutical
companies have made much greater commitments to gene and cell therapy than their US counterparts, spending some $1.4 billion on alliances
and acquisitions compared with $150 million by American companies as
of December 1996 (see Tables 8.5 and 8.6). In addition, four large US
biotechnology firms have also invested over $200 million in gene therapy,
although it is interesting that two of these, Genentech and Chiron, are
controlled by European pharmaceutical companies.

The most striking feature of the 32 alliances and acquisitions listed in
these tables is that only three are with European gene therapy firms
(Transgene, IntroGene and CellGenix), suggesting that nearly all the pharmaceutical industry's investment in gene therapy is being made in the US.

It is difficult to estimate the scale of pharmaceutical companies' own
in-house research on gene therapy, but anecdotal evidence suggests that it
is far smaller than that being made by gene therapy firms themselves.
These partnerships therefore represent the main way in which large firms
are obtaining access to gene therapy technology.

Commercial Support and Sponsorship of Clinical Trials

A striking difference between the US and Europe is the extent to which
companies are involved in the clinical development of gene therapy.
Clinical trials are the main way in which clinical development occurs, and
they can be sponsored either by academic researchers or by companies.
However, in order to gain regulatory approval for their products, companies must sponsor their own clinical trials. Nearly all the 207 clinical
trials of gene therapy in Europe and the US are early stage (Phase I/II),
with 175 sponsored by academic groups and 32 directly sponsored by
firms. At the end of 1996, European firms were sponsoring only five
clinical trials, compared with 27 by US firms, thus demonstrating the lead
US firms have in developing commercial products.

Table 8.5   Alliances with US pharmaceutical and large biotechnology companies (December 1996)

Company	Partner	Investment	Disease area
Pharmaceutical companies			
Baxter	Somatix	Undisclosed	Haemophilia and CGD[1]
	Vical	Undisclosed	Haemophilia
Bristol-Myers			
Squibb	Somatix	Up to $30m	Cancer
Pfizer	Megabios	Up to $50m	Cancer
Schering Plough	Canji	Acquired for $55m	
	Human Genome Sciences	Undisclosed	Gene discovery for gene therapy
Biotechnology companies			
Biogen	Genovo	Up to $35m	Lung and liver diseases
Chiron	Viagene	Acquired for $95m	
	Progenitor	Up to $50m	Cancer
Genentech	GenVec	$17m	Cystic fibrosis
	Cytotherapeutics	$11m	Alzheimer's
Genzyme	GeneMedicine	$2m	
	Vical	Undisclosed	Cystic fibrosis
	IntroGene	Undisclosed	Gaucher's

Note: 1. Chronic Granulomatous Disease.

In addition, companies often support early stage academic trials in order to obtain access to technology and gain experience of clinical development.[9] In the US some 75 per cent of all trials have firms involved, compared with 50 per cent in Europe (Martin and Thomas, 1996, p. 59). However, half of the European trials supported by companies involve American firms, a quarter involve large pharmaceutical companies and only a quarter involve European gene therapy firms. In contrast, almost all US trials with commercial support involve US dedicated gene therapy firms. These figures demonstrate that the science base in Europe is less industrially exploited than in the US, and indicates that many of the commercial benefits from European clinical research may go to US firms. Part of the explanation for this is the greater maturity of the US gene therapy industry, which is more clinically focused. In addition, however, there are probably too few dedicated European firms in this area, allowing US gene therapy firms to take advantage of the lack of competition.

Table 8.6 Alliances with European pharmaceutical companies (December 1996)

Company	Partner	Investment	Disease area
Astra	Cytotherapeutics	Up to $41m	Chronic pain
Bayer	Viagene	Up to $9m	Haemophilia
	Immune Response	Up to $10m	Haemophilia
Boehringer	GeneMedicine	Up to $100m	Cancer
Mannheim	CellPro	$30m	Cell separation devices
Glaxo Wellcome	Megabios	Undisclosed	Cystic fibrosis
Groupe Fournier	RGene	Up to $25m	Tumour suppressers
Hoechst	Cell Genesys	Up to $50m	HIV
	Transkaryotic Therapies	At least $5m	Undisclosed
Roche	GeneMedicine	Up to $70m	Inflammation
RPR	Transgene	Equity	Adenoviral vectors
	Genetix	Undisclosed	Vectors
	Introgen	Up to $50m	Cancer
	AIS	Acquired for total of $220m	
	AASTROM	Up to $25m	Cell processing
Sandoz	Genetic Therapy	Acquired for $290m	
	Systemix	Owns 72% for total of $470m[1]	
Schering AG	CellGenix	Metreon joint venture	Cell processing

Note: 1. Sandoz has made an offer for the remaining shares in the company, but this transaction was not finalized as of December 1996.

Exploitation of the European Science Base

Taken as a whole these indicators suggest that while Europe has a strong science base in gene therapy, it has lagged three to five years behind the US in both clinical and commercial development. It now has an emerging gene therapy industry, but US firms are more numerous, larger, closer to developing products and more integrated into the pharmaceutical industry than their European counterparts. This has encouraged European pharmaceutical companies to invest in the US rather than directly in Europe. Furthermore, the smaller size of the European gene therapy industry has also led to a significant number of European investigators involved in clinical trials to collaborate with US firms. It therefore appears that although European investigators are rapidly developing the technology and large firms are investing in the field, the lack of small European gene therapy companies is forcing both groups to work with the US gene therapy industry.

Evidence to support this analysis, and a more detailed explanation follow in the next section, which summarizes the case study of the development of gene therapy in the UK and US.

A COMPARATIVE ANALYSIS OF THE GENE THERAPY INNOVATION SYSTEMS IN THE US AND UK

The purpose of the detailed comparative case study of gene therapy in the UK and the US was to examine the role of the main groups involved in the innovation process in a systematic manner and then to use this to highlight key differences between the US and UK. In particular, this section examines the activities of each of the four principal groups involved: academic researchers, regulators, clinicians and firms.[10]

Comparing Basic Research in the US and UK

Basic research on gene transfer is essential for the development of gene therapy and, as mentioned above, the US produces some 60 per cent of all gene therapy-related scientific papers compared with the 8 per cent published by UK authors. However, UK researchers publish roughly the same share of papers on gene therapy as they do in biomedical research as a whole. Furthermore, the overall impression given by interviews with both domestic and US investigators was that UK basic research was world class and internationally competitive, but the extent to which this work was commercially exploited differed.

The most important reason for the difference in the number of publications between the US and the UK is the sheer scale of US biomedical research. The US spends about ten times more than the UK on gene therapy research ($300–400 million compared with $40 million), with roughly equal amounts being spent by government and industry (Martin and Thomas, 1996, p. 22). Public sector research is concentrated in a relatively small number of national institutes, medical schools and cancer centres in both countries and the top US research institutes working on gene therapy are very much larger than any UK centre. A significant number of spin-off firms have been founded from these leading centres in the US and it may be that a critical mass of research is needed to support the creation of a new firm. Given that UK institutes are much smaller, this may be one factor in the relatively low number of gene therapy firms in the UK.

Policies to promote the development of gene therapy in the US have been largely uncoordinated and there have been few calls for the National Institutes of Health (NIH) to play a greater role. In contrast, UK national policy is steered by a Medical Research Council (MRC) coordinating committee, which involves many of the key groups in the innovation process. UK interviewees were generally supportive of the MRC's role, but a significant number felt there needed to be more investment in gene therapy research, that other UK government departments should give more attention to the field and that problems associated with getting access to vector production facilities had to be overcome. It would therefore appear that national policy and government coordination of the innovation process have not been factors in the success of the US in developing gene therapy. However, heavy Federal investment in basic research has certainly been very significant. In contrast, policy coordination is important if the UK is to catch up with the US.

Bioethics, Regulation and the Public Acceptability of Gene Therapy

Despite a long-running debate about the ethics of somatic gene therapy in the US, there is now broad public support for its development. This has been achieved, in part, through a policy of closely scrutinizing the ethical problems it presents and open public discussion of these issues. Somatic gene therapy has provoked far less controversy in the UK and also commands general public acceptance. However, in both the US and UK there is strong opposition to any moves towards the introduction of germ-line therapy and there still remain some residual concerns about the safety and ethics of somatic therapy. These reservations are not surprising given the nature of this technology, the controversies surrounding biotechnology in general and the long history of social anxiety concerning eugenics.

An important mechanism for ensuring continued public and professional support for gene therapy has been national oversight of clinical research, which is a common feature of the US and the UK. In both countries this review process is unique to gene therapy, and is in addition to local ethical review and the work of the agencies regulating new medicines. While the research oversight function in the US has at times been criticized for being slow and time consuming, it has been streamlined and is now generally supported[11] (Martin and Thomas, 1996, p. 43). In the UK, the work of the oversight body, the Gene Therapy Advisory Committee has not been criticized, other than for holding its meetings in private, and is also broadly supported by researchers. Overall, the barrier to innovation posed by the oversight of clinical research does not appear to be a major factor slowing the development of gene therapy in either country. Other issues are probably more important in inhibiting clinical development, as witnessed by the fact that in March 1996 nearly half the approved US trials had yet to commence.

Another way in which public confidence in new therapies is maintained is through the tight control of new medicinal products by the Food and Drug Administration (FDA) in the US and the Medicines Control Agency (MCA) in the UK. Gene therapy is being regulated as a novel biological product in both countries and as such has been accommodated into the existing framework for new biological drugs. Regulatory policies and practices are better established in the US than the UK, probably reflecting the different rates of commercialization of the technology. The situation in the UK is complicated by the adoption of a new Europe-wide approval process for biotechnology products, which is still in its infancy. In the US there has been some frustration about the general workings of the FDA in terms of the burden it places on industry, but there was no specific criticism from gene therapy firms of its activities relating specifically to gene therapy. No such criticisms of the MCA/European Medicines Evaluation Agency were recorded in the UK. It would therefore appear that while government regulation of new medicinal products is a very significant hurdle in the innovation process, there is no extra barrier for gene therapy in this respect and no major differences between the US and UK.

Clinical development

The organization of clinical trials is the key step in taking promising laboratory techniques and reducing them to clinical practice. By June 1996, some 161 trials of gene therapy had been approved or started in the US compared with 14 in the UK. This is roughly in line with the number of scientific papers produced, and the amount spent on gene therapy-related research, by each country. In addition, broadly similar therapeutic strategies and disease targets are being investigated in both countries. There is no significant difference in the institutional base for these trials, with most being organized in national medical research institutes, medical schools and specialist hospitals. Overall, it would therefore appear that the pattern of clinical development of gene therapy is very similar in the US and UK, and no specific differences were identified by interviewees.

Investigators in both countries highlighted common barriers to the clinical development of gene therapy, with most believing that the greatest obstacles to the introduction of the technology were technical. In particular, the need for more efficient targetable vectors was seen as a key requirement. However, a number of other non-technical problems relating to clinical development were also thought to account for the fact that only about half the approved trials had commenced. Getting final regulatory approval from the FDA or MCA and access to clinical grade vector production and other key technologies, were given as the main reasons for these delays.

Vector production is complex and expensive, and the creation of dedicated scale facilities is beyond the means of almost all academic institutions. Clinical investigators are mainly dependent on purchasing clinical grade vector production from either dedicated gene therapy firms or a small number of contract manufacturers. The capacity of the gene therapy industry to support vector production for academic research is limited by the small number of established production facilities. Many gene therapy companies also require investigators to enter into formal agreements in return for access to vector production, thus giving them rights to exploit the research commercially. As a consequence clinical research is being limited by access to vector production and increasingly tied into firms at a very early stage. This constrains the freedom of investigators and channels publicly funded research in particular directions, and has led to calls in the US, UK and Europe for publicly funded vector production. Both the NIH and MRC are currently trying to establish such facilities.

The conflict between public research and the commercial interests of industry is also highlighted by evidence from the US which suggests that other key technologies, owned by firms through patents and essential to clinical trials, were not always being made available to academic investigators. This was particularly true where the research might benefit other firms or where the risk of an adverse reaction during the trial would be commercially damaging. In an attempt to tackle this problem, the NIH has recently recommended the implementation of mechanisms to facilitate the distribution and testing of vectors and adjunct materials for use in clinical studies.

Commercial Development

The major difference between the US and the UK is the overall level and pattern of commercial development of gene therapy. The US has a higher intensity of academic–industry collaborations, more dedicated gene therapy firms, and greater exploitation of its science base by both local and foreign pharmaceutical companies and biotechnology firms.

The extent to which academic researchers are working with companies provides one indicator of the commercialization of the science bases. Of the 13 principal investigators interviewed in the US, ten had founded, and were collaborating with local gene therapy companies, while in the UK only one of the 12 principal investigators interviewed was involved in a gene therapy firm and a further two had collaborations with the US biotechnology company, Genzyme. The other nine researchers had no direct involvement with firms commercializing gene therapy. In addition, only three of the 14 UK clinical trials (that is, <25 per cent) are supported by companies, compared with over 75 per cent of trials in the US. This suggests that the UK science base is being less exploited than its US counterpart.

Another important indicator of the commercial development of gene therapy is the number of small firms working on the technology. In the US there are some 16 dedicated gene therapy firms, six cell therapy firms working on gene therapy, and four other biopharmaceutical companies sponsoring gene therapy clinical trials. In the UK there is one established gene therapy company,[12] no cell therapy firms and no UK biopharmaceutical firms sponsoring gene therapy clinical trials. This is a surprisingly small number given that the UK has the largest number of biotechnology small and medium-sized enterprises in Europe: it might be expected to have two or three gene or cell therapy firms considering the level of basic research and the number of clinical trials.

There is also some evidence to suggest that large pharmaceutical companies and foreign biotechnology firms are playing a much greater role in the direct commercialization of gene therapy in the UK compared with the US. First, there is one UK clinical trial supported by a UK pharmaceutical company (Glaxo Wellcome) and two trials supported by foreign firms (Boehringer Mannheim and Genzyme). To date no trials have been supported by either a UK biotechnology or gene therapy firm. In contrast, none of the US trials examined were supported by either large pharmaceutical companies or foreign firms. Second, larger companies are also significant in the pattern of academic–industry collaborations in the UK. While in the US the academic researchers interviewed worked exclusively with small domestic biotechnology and gene therapy firms, in the UK investigators tended to collaborate with pharmaceutical companies and US biotechnology firms, in particular Genzyme. Of the 11 academic–industry gene therapy collaborations identified in the UK, two were with the UK gene therapy firm Therexsys, two were with UK pharmaceutical companies, five were with the US biotechnology company

Genzyme, and a further two were with other foreign firms. Significantly, Genzyme has also signed an important commercialization agreement for gene therapy research with the UK's Imperial Cancer Research Fund.

This evidence suggests that there is both a lower level of exploitation of the UK science base and a different pattern of commercial development compared with the US. Not only is the potential of UK basic research not being realized, but where research is being exploited many of the commercial benefits are going to foreign rather than domestic firms.

The lower level of commercial exploitation of the UK science base in gene therapy compared with the US

One of the most obvious explanations for this lower level of commercial exploitation is that research in the UK is less advanced, having started some years after the US. This does not, however, fully explain the lack of academic–industry links, many of which are concerned with early-stage basic research, nor why so few Phase I clinical trials involve companies. Another reason often cited as contributing to the lack of commercial exploitation of basic research is that UK academics are less commercially oriented than in the US. However, this view was not supported in gene therapy since most UK investigators in the field hold patents and are keen to work with industry.

There is, however, a significant difference between technology transfer mechanisms in the US and the UK which may influence the level of commercial exploitation. Formal institutional technology transfer mechanisms, such as the use of Cooperative Research and Development Agreements and Technology Transfer Offices, appear to be more established in the US than in the UK, and these have undoubtedly facilitated the industrial exploitation of basic research. However, the most important mechanism for technology transfer in the US is the creation of small dedicated gene therapy firms, most of which have been 'spun-off' from research institutions or been co-founded by academics. This is not a general feature of biomedical innovation in the UK; instead direct links with large pharmaceutical companies have traditionally played a greater role in transferring technology from the laboratory. In this respect it is interesting to note that several UK investigators expressed frustration at the lack of interest from established British companies in their research, and this had been a reason for them working with small US firms.

Large UK pharmaceutical companies have only recently started to invest in gene therapy either internally or through external linkages, and have made fewer commitments than many of their European counterparts. Several investigators commented that large firms were more cautious about the prospects for gene therapy and generally preferred to invest in a small start-up company rather than directly supporting academic groups, as these firms already have intellectual property and are commercially focused. This view is supported by research on the reasons behind pharmaceutical companies' external linkages (Senker, Joly and Reinhard, 1996).

The different pattern of commercial development in the UK and US

One of the most important differences between the US and UK is the number of dedicated gene therapy firms. The later development of gene therapy in the UK is undoubtedly a contributing factor. For example, the first UK gene therapy firm, Therexsys, was founded six years after the first US company. The much smaller scale of basic research in the UK is also less able to support the creation of new firms. However, these factors alone do not explain the lower ratio of gene therapy firms to clinical trials or scientific publications in the UK, or why large pharmaceutical companies and foreign biotechnology firms are exploiting basic research in the UK.

A more likely explanation lies in the difficulties of starting a new biotechnology firm in Britain (Walsh, Niosi and Mustar, 1995). Interviews with academic researchers and managers involved in the gene therapy industry suggest that starting a biotechnology firm is much easier in the US than in the UK. The founding of dedicated gene therapy firms in the US and the UK was therefore compared to see if any differences in the process of firm creation could be identified.

Company executives were asked about how their firm was started and, in particular, who had taken the initiative to establish the company. Of the eight American firms for which information is available, researchers were involved in initiating the creation of six firms, venture capitalists of four firms and existing biotechnology companies of three dedicated firms. In the four cases where venture capitalists were involved directly, they played the leading role by either funding basic research or bringing other people together to create the company. In two cases, dedicated firms were created as spin-offs from existing biotechnology companies. In contrast, the creation of the only established UK firm, Therexsys, was initiated by two researchers and an experienced manager from the pharmaceutical industry, with support from the MRC and Cancer Research Campaign UK.

Managers and researchers involved in the creation of biotechnology firms in the UK were asked for their views about the main barriers to the commercial exploitation of gene therapy in Britain and the main differences between company creation in the UK and the US. Five main differences between the US and the UK were highlighted:

1. Easier access to seed capital in the US Dr Roger Craig, one of the founders of Therexsys told an MRC conference on 'Successful Exploitation of Biomedical Research' (Craig, 1994) that the hardest part of founding Therexsys was raising the initial £400 000 seed capital.[13] He is also on record as saying that it would have been much easier to start Therexsys in the US than in the UK. Other respondents also commented on the difficulty there was in raising seed capital for UK start-up biotechnology firms. This view has been supported by research carried out by the Bank of England, which also highlighted the greater role played by business angels in providing seed finance (Bank of England, 1996). In addition, a survey of biotechnology firms in the UK found that only about one in five firms received venture capital, with most companies founded with the entrepreneur's personal savings (Walsh, Niosi and Mustar, 1995). In contrast, in the US it is much more common for start-up firms to be financed by venture capital (Walsh, Niosi and Mustar, 1995).

2. A more active role played by American venture capitalists in the creation of firms One interviewee with experience of trying to establish a number of biotechnology firms in the UK considered that many American venture capitalists were more proactive in establishing new companies. In general, it appears that scientists and entrepreneurs have to approach UK venture capital funds with ideas, whereas in the US venture capitalists often play the lead role in initiating a new firm. This view is supported by the fact that in the founding of four of the eight American gene therapy firms examined, it was the venture capitalists who took the initiative. This difference may also be due to the greater size of the American venture capital industry, although the structure of the industry may also be a factor. In the UK, the main venture funds are associated with large city institutions, whereas in America there are a number of regional funds, smaller private funds and venture capital partnerships which are perhaps more entrepreneurial. Other research gives weight to this view, where it is argued that the whole process of commercialization of biotechnology was initiated by venture capitalists, who identified commercial opportunities, scientists and premises (Florida and Kenney, 1988).

3. Financial incentives and government support for high technology companies in the US Four respondents commented on the much greater financial support which was available to assist the creation of new biotechnology companies in the US compared with the UK. This is also highlighted by the Bank of England study which concludes that the US government, 'plays a more active role in the development and financing of technology-based firms than in the United Kingdom' (Bank of

England, 1996, p. 47). In particular, tax breaks to encourage investment, free rents, grants for building factories and other forms of incentive are used by a number of US states to attract high technology firms. Nothing comparable exists in the UK. However, in both countries, small grants are available to companies to assist their development. One unique form of support for the biotechnology industry in the US has been the network of nearly 100 local biotechnology centres which have been established to promote the development of biotechnology in a defined geographical area. Collectively these centres employ over 2000 staff, spend some $270 million, and it is estimated that they have helped start some 165 biotechnology firms (Dibner, 1995).

Similar national and regional support is available to help new biotechnology firms in some European countries. In particular, three of the four recently established German gene therapy firms have received grants to help their foundation from either the local *Land* or Federal government (Unterhuber and Furst, 1996). This support may explain the greater number of German gene therapy firms compared with other EU countries.

4. A lack of entrepreneurs in the UK Another issue of concern was the apparent lack of entrepreneurs or experienced managers from the pharmaceutical industry willing to take the risk of setting up a small biotechnology firm. While evidence for this point is anecdotal, it is interesting to note that many US biotechnology companies have been established with British managers. One explanation for this is simply that UK managers with an interest in starting or running a biotechnology firm have been attracted to the US, where the opportunities in the biotechnology industry are much greater.

Two leading UK scientists also commented that it was much harder for British academics to be involved in founding firms, as little recognition or support for the creation of companies was given by universities. In particular, sabbaticals and time off from teaching commitments would help greatly and it was suggested that funds could be made available to help make this possible.

5. A large and more mature biotechnology industry in the US Several company executives in the US spontaneously commented that they felt it was probably easier to found a firm in the US compared with Europe. One reason they gave for this was the size and maturity of the American biotechnology industry, which provided an infrastructure to support the creation and development of firms. In particular, the large number of existing companies, financial institutions with experience of biotechnology, analysts and business consultants working in the area, a large number of potential suppliers, experienced staff and a rich science base were all seen as providing a critical mass which enabled the commercialization of gene therapy. It is worth noting that three existing US biotechnology companies were involved in the creation of gene therapy firms, something which would be much more difficult to achieve in the UK given the small size of the domestic biotechnology sector.

It therefore appears that there are strong institutional reasons why it is easier to start a new biotechnology firm in the US than the UK. These undoubtedly go some way to explaining why there are only a few UK firms working on gene therapy.

The other main feature of the commercialization of gene therapy in the UK, the greater role played by large pharmaceutical companies and foreign biotechnology firms, is probably also a reflection of this lack of small UK biotechnology and gene therapy firms. There are simply not enough dedicated gene therapy firms in the UK to support the commercialization of the UK science base, and investigators are having to work with other sections of the biopharmaceutical industry instead.

It would therefore appear that both the low level of exploitation of the science base and the greater role of foreign firms in the UK can be largely accounted for by the lack of effective means for transferring technology from basic research institutions to the pharmaceutical industry. While formal mechanisms are important, the most effective way this has been achieved in the US is through the creation of small dedicated gene therapy firms. These companies, often founded by researchers, have taken basic research and transformed it into potential products in early clinical trials, and are now being rapidly integrated into the pharmaceutical industry. They function, in effect, as technology transfer intermediaries. The lack of a larger population of dedicated firms in the UK has led to both a significant number of basic researchers working with foreign companies and European pharmaceutical companies making investments in the US rather than the UK. In this sense, there is what might be called a 'commercialization gap' in the UK which prevents it from fully realizing the potential of its science base.

Comparing the Overall Structure of the US and UK Innovation Systems

The main similarities and differences between the overall features of the US and UK innovation systems can be summarized as follows:

- *Basic research*. This is organized in very similar ways in both countries. However, the main difference is one of scale, with the US publishing eight times as many scientific papers and spending ten times as much on gene therapy research as the UK. The leading US research institutes are very much bigger than any UK centre. Unlike the UK, national policy in the US has been largely uncoordinated.
- *Bioethics and regulation*. Broad consent exists for somatic therapy in both countries. The oversight of clinical research and the regulation of new medicinal products are also organized in a similar manner.
- *Clinical development*. The process and organization of clinical development is essentially the same in the US and the UK. As with basic research, the main difference is scale, with some ten times as many clinical trials in the US.
- *Commercial development*. There is less commercial exploitation of the science base in the UK than in the US. In addition, there are fewer small dedicated gene therapy firms than might have been expected, and greater involvement of foreign firms in commercially developing basic research, than in the US. These differences are accounted for by the lack of effective technology transfer mechanisms and barriers to the creation of biotechnology firms in the UK.

Although the development of gene therapy in the US is more advanced and conducted on a much larger scale than in the UK, the only systemic difference is in the area of commercial development. It would appear that the central strength of the US gene therapy innovation system compared with that in the UK is its ability to create small firms to transfer technology efficiently from the laboratory to industry.

It is striking that this analysis of the UK and US innovation systems fits well with the overall comparison of the US and Europe made in the previous section. Given that there appears to be a 'commercialization gap' in both the UK and Europe as a whole, this suggests that the study of the UK is valuable in highlighting key issues for other EU member states.

CONCLUSIONS

This comparative study indicates that the pattern of commercial development of gene therapy in the UK and the rest of Europe is marked by a number of significant features:

- commercialization lags a number of years behind the US;
- a lower level of exploitation of the science base compared with the US;
- a relatively smaller number of dedicated gene therapy firms;
- the significant involvement of US firms in supporting clinical development;
- heavy investment by large European pharmaceutical companies in the US gene therapy industry and very little investment in Europe.

Drawing on the UK experience, it appears that this situation can be explained by the lack of effective technology transfer mechanisms and the small number of spin-off firms. There are several important conclusions which arise from this analysis:

- The commercial potential of the European science base is not being fully realized.
- US firms are benefiting as much as European companies from European research into gene therapy.
- The European gene therapy industry is small and lags behind US firms.
- By investing heavily in the US, European pharmaceutical companies are strengthening the US biotechnology industry and helping to create high value jobs in America rather than Europe.
- European pharmaceutical companies are acquiring a very significant commercial advantage over their US counterparts in the field of gene therapy by controlling a large amount of the US industry.

A paradox is therefore presented, in that considerable benefits from European basic research are going to small US firms, but these are in turn being acquired by large European pharmaceutical companies. The overall long-term costs and benefits of this situation are unclear for European states, as the creation of jobs in the US biotechnology industry may be offset by the increase in competitiveness of the European pharmaceutical sector.[14]

However, public policy should act to improve on this situation by strengthening the commercial development of gene therapy in Europe. This would ensure that a greater socio-economic return could be realized from public research, that more European jobs could be created and that the overall competitiveness of the European biotechnology industry could be enhanced. The ways in which this could be done include improving technology transfer mechanisms, reducing the barriers to commercialization and assisting the creation of new biotechnology enterprises. Specific proposals to close the 'commercialization gap' might include:

1. *Improving technology transfer and increasing academic–industry links.*
   Coherent national policies to promote technology transfer in biomedical research in general, and gene therapy in particular, are needed to
   help the commercialization of the European science base. EU member
   states should introduce comprehensive policies to improve technology
   transfer in the field of gene therapy, including greater funding for
   local technology transfer mechanisms, such as institution-based technology transfer offices; creating legal frameworks to encourage
   technology transfer and commercialization; introducing measures to
   promote collaborative research with industrial partners; and increasing incentives for scientists to exploit their research.

2. *Stimulating the creation of new gene therapy firms.* Within the US gene
   therapy innovation system there is a large number of small dedicated
   gene therapy firms, which in effect function as technology transfer
   intermediaries between the science base and the pharmaceutical
   industry. A key part of any strategy to improve the commercialization
   of European research would be to foster the creation of a greater
   number of these dedicated firms. European governments should
   therefore seek to improve the support given to the creation of new
   biotechnology enterprises. Specifically, these policies could include:

   - measures to increase the availability of seed capital and long-term
     finance;
   - fiscal incentives to encourage investment in new firms and R&D;
   - regional government support, such as is available in France and
     Germany, in the form of grants and financial guarantees;
   - the creation of technology centres and 'incubator facilities', and
     increased technical assistance and management support;
   - provision of greater opportunities to academic investigators who
     would like to start their own firm. In particular, the funding of sab-
     baticals and time off to start and manage new firms are essential.

It is possible that gene therapy is an exception in being relatively under-
exploited. However, anecdotal evidence suggests that the same pattern
exists in other leading-edge biotechnologies, including the development of
genomics, cell therapies, antisense oligonucleotides, combinatorial chemistry and, to a lesser extent, transgenics. For example, in human genomics
there are some ten well-established US firms working in this area, compared with just one established firm in Europe. The commercialization gap
identified in this study may therefore be a more general phenomenon,[15] in
which case it has major implications for European technology, industrial
and employment policy. Further research on this subject and the develop-

ment of coherent public policies to improve the commercial exploitation of Europe's rich science base are urgently needed.

NOTES

1. There are two types of gene therapy. Somatic gene therapy targets the non-reproductive cells and therefore only affects the patient treated. In contrast, germ-line gene therapy alters the reproductive cells and thus changes future generations. At present only somatic therapy is being developed.
2. Martin and Thomas (1996).
3. These techniques are applied through the use of gene transfer systems or vectors, which often involve the use of modified viruses to transfer the therapeutic gene to the target tissue.
4. However, it is unclear if gene therapies will be any less toxic than any other form of therapeutic.
5. *Ex-vivo* gene therapy involves the genetic modification of a patient's cells outside the body, that is, they are removed, modified and returned to the patient in a fashion similar to bone marrow transplantation. In contrast, *in-vivo* gene therapy involves the direct application of the therapy to the patient and is similar to a conventional drug.
6. According to the US National Science Board, US researchers published 39 per cent of all biomedical research publications in 1991, while the share for European authors was 32 per cent (National Science Board, 1993).
7. Five of the gene and cell therapy firms have recently been acquired by large pharmaceutical companies or other gene therapy firms.
8. Genzyme, for example, is spending over $30 million a year on gene therapy research, more than any dedicated gene therapy firm.
9. Support can take a number of forms, including finance, the supply of technology or the production of vectors.
10. The results are based on over 50 interviews with academic investigators, clinicians, regulatory agencies and firm managers.
11. In May 1996 the Director of NIH proposed to abolish its Recombinant DNA Advisory Committee, but this was strongly opposed in the scientific community and has been subsequently withdrawn.
12. A second firm, Oxford BioMedica, was founded in the summer of 1996 and floated on the Alternative Investment Market in December 1996.
13. The subsequent round of private financing for Therexsys was apparently much easier to organize. It raised some £6 million and was substantially oversubscribed.
14. It may also be the case that being a later entrant into the field has advantages, in that European firms can avoid being locked into the first generations of gene delivery technologies and can better exploit more recent vector systems. Although US firms are in a commanding patent position on *ex-vivo* therapies, there appears to be no blocking patents in the *in-vivo* field preventing European firms from entering this area.
15. This would not be surprising given the conclusion reached in this study, namely that there is a 'systemic' difference between the US and Europe in the way in which technology is transferred and small biotechnology firms are founded.

REFERENCES

Bank of England (1996), *The Financing of Technology-Based Small Firms*, London: Bank of England.
Craig, R. (1994), *Exploitation of LCR Technology*, Presentation to MRC confer-

ence on the successful exploitation of biomedical research, 7–8 March, Regents College, London.

Dibner, M. (1995), 'Biotech centers represent a major force in development and support of industry', *Genetic Engineering News*, **15**(17), 4.

Florida, R.L. and M. Kenney (1988), 'Venture capital-financed innovation and technological change in the USA', *Research Policy*, **17**(3), 119–37.

Martin, P.A. (1995), 'The American gene therapy industry and the social shaping of a new technology', *The Genetic Engineer and Biotechnologist*, **15**, 155.

Martin, P.A. and S.M. Thomas (1996), *The Development of Gene Therapy in Europe and the United States: A Comparative Analysis*. STEEP Special Report No. 5, Brighton: Science Policy Research Unit, University of Sussex.

National Science Board (1993), *Science and Engineering Indicators – 1993*, Washington, DC: US Government Printing Office.

Senker, J., P.-B. Joly and M. Reinhard (1996), *Overseas Biotechnology Research by Europe's Chemical/Pharmaceuticals Multinationals: Rationale and Implications*, Final Report for the Biotechnology Programme (BIOTECH) of the European Community, DG XII, STEEP Discussion Paper No. 33, Brighton: Science Policy Research Unit, University of Sussex.

Unterhuber, R.J. and I.E. Furst (1996), 'Gene therapy goes commercial in Germany with entrance of startup firms', *Genetic Engineering News*, **15**(3), 1.

Walsh, V., J. Niosi and P. Mustar (1995), 'Small-firm formation in biotechnology: a comparison of France, Britain and Canada', *Technovation*, **15**(9), 303–27.

9. Conclusions: biotechnology and European competitiveness

Rohini Acharya[1]

INTRODUCTION

The relative success or failure of countries to establish commercial biotechnology has been dependent on a wide range of factors. Some relate to the external development environment in which firms function. In the case of biotechnology, the science base and, in particular, the strengths and weaknesses of the country's science base, have often determined the strengths and weaknesses of commercial biotechnology and the particular development paths followed by firms.[2] The conditions of market entry, determined by the state of the regulatory and financial environment as well as industrial structure, are also important reasons for the particular path taken by commercial biotechnology in several countries.

The goal of this book was to examine the scientific and commercial development of biotechnology in Europe, to contrast its experiences with that of the technological leader, the US, and to understand why Europe has fallen behind in applications of the technology, when its scientific capabilities are largely comparable with those in the US. The chapters have emphasized major differences between the US and European countries in terms of differences in market entry conditions mentioned above. One of the main focuses in many of the studies was the role played by the dedicated biotechnology firm (DBF), which was created in the US in the early 1980s. Its success in commercializing biotechnology in the US, and its relative absence until recently in European countries, has often led to the conclusion that Europe was perhaps slower to commercialize biotechnology because of the smaller presence of such DBFs. The projects set out to examine the role of the DBF in Europe which is considerably different from that in the US, and its relationship to other major actors in the R&D community, such as the multinational companies (MNCs) which have played a much more important role in Europe than in the US, the science base, and the business and financial community.

THE EXTERNAL ENVIRONMENT: HOW IMPORTANT IS IT?

The external environment for the purposes of this project was defined as the policy, regulatory and institutional factors that affect the development of firms and their ability to innovate and be competitive. In the case of a technology such as biotechnology, which is strongly rooted in basic science, the strengthening of the science base forms an obvious starting point for policy, but as firms have developed over the years, other factors such as access to finance, patenting and regulation regarding the release of genetically engineered material into the environment have become equally important.

Chapter 2 presented an overview of this environment and its evolution, arguing that the policies adopted by many European countries reflected the concerns of policy makers and industrialists that Europe was falling behind in applications of biotechnology, and aimed to develop an environment in which the science base could be strengthened, cooperation could be increased between scientific and commercial actors and, in particular, the small DBF could flourish. The programmes themselves were of course different across countries, placing an emphasis on previous traditions of scientific research and collaboration and conditions of market entry. The domination of biotechnology by large multinational companies (MNCs) in several European countries, notably Germany, also focused policies on public R&D programmes in these countries.

The main problem facing Europe, however, was the different approaches to the regulation of biotechnology R&D. Significant differences existed, and continue to exist, between countries such as Denmark and Germany, for example, which have indicated a preference for more stringent regulations concerning the release of genetically engineered organisms into the atmosphere, and countries such as France, the Netherlands and the United Kingdom, which prefer somewhat less stringent regulations. In preparing its directives on the contained use of genetically modified organisms (GMOs) and their deliberate release, the European Commission has had to find a compromise between these diverging views. The result has often been criticism of these directives from policy makers in both groups of countries and from industry and environmental activists, who also often do not share the same views on this subject. The European biotechnology industry is asking for an amendment to these directives, arguing that their stringency is not good for the competitiveness of European biotechnology and also calling for greater transparency in the implementation procedure. The debate on regulation in Europe has also been perceived to be disadvantageous because of the apparent uncertainty it creates for European firms and also non-European firms that wish to locate in Europe.

This is not to say, however, that Europe has been unable or unwilling to address this issue. One area where Europe is perhaps ahead of the US is in the regulation of medical products through the European Medicines Evaluation Agency, which approves products based on their safety, a quicker process than through the Federal Drugs Administration, which also has to prove that the products are efficacious. However, while regulatory approval may be relatively faster in Europe, the process of obtaining approval by individual member states for the price of the product is still needed in Europe, adding another stage to the approval process (Ward, 1995, 1996).

The complexity of the regulatory and approval process, as well as its evolution over time, was the subject of Chapter 4 on the regulation of agricultural biotechnologies. Over the years, disagreements between governments, non-governmental organizations (NGOs) and industry over the possible environmental consequences of too little regulation and the equally possible and negative consequences of too much regulation on European competitiveness have often been bitter and protracted. The study, however, found that over time, a combination of factors, including pressure from other countries which have continued to approve biotechnology products and international agreements, have resulted in the worst fears of the environmentalists not being realized, and a growing number of groups believe that there may be room for compromise. Industrialists, NGOs and policy makers alike appear to believe that fast track and other solutions can be found within the existing procedures to strike a balance between the need for protecting the environment from the possible negative consequences of GMO release and for improving the competitiveness of Europe's biotechnology industry. Industrialists themselves have been more willing to work with new issues such as labelling, showing a shift towards an adaptive strategy on the part of industry, rather than technocratic solutions.

INDUSTRIAL STRUCTURES: CONTRASTS BETWEEN EUROPE AND THE US

While the first part of this book presented the main policy and regulatory environments in Europe and the challenges faced by policy makers in adapting their policies to the varying and changing needs of their populations, the second part dealt more closely with issues of commercialization and industrial structure.

The general industrial structure that has developed in Europe was first discussed and contrasted with that in the US, in Chapter 3. The development of industrial biotechnology in Europe and the US has been facilitated by the interactions between the science base, small firms or new entrants, and the large incumbents that have dominated the European market more than that of the US. In general, while the industrial environment has displayed considerable turbulence over the years, the entry of DBFs has been complementary to the activities of incumbents, rather than displacing them altogether. Collaboration, in addition to competition, has often helped small DBFs to enter the market and maintain their position, sometimes simply as suppliers of niche market products. Other DBFs have been more successful in deepening and widening their technological base over the years, becoming more established in the R&D network in the process.

The role of the DBF in Europe has also been considerably different from that in the US, reflecting the different structures and relationships in the European scientific and business community.

Given the tendency to focus on the role of the DBF when comparing biotechnology in Europe and the US, Chapters 5 and 6 looked at the DBF and its contribution to biotechnology in Europe. Chapter 5 first examined the process by which the DBF was formed in Europe. Although the DBF was relatively absent in the 1980s in Europe, this is no longer the case, and while the US may still lead in terms of the absolute numbers of firms, the relative growth of DBFs has been faster in Europe (Department of Trade and Industry, 1995). Rather, it is the technology gap between European and American firms which remains large, leaving European biotechnology at a disadvantage *vis-à-vis* its competitors in the US. Indeed the study found that large, diversified firms in Europe appeared to have a preference for purchasing US and not European DBFs, demonstrating perhaps greater confidence in US DBFs and also the regulatory and technological environment in the US, although these results were not conclusive.

Technology gaps appear to be emerging in certain fields such as genetic therapy and antisense technology, which are at the forefront of modern techniques and where firms in the US seem to have a clear lead. Evidence of a technology gap as being the major reason for European biotechnology lagging behind the US was also found in Chapter 6, which examined the evolution over time of the European biotechnology network. While the US network, as would be expected, is significantly larger and older than the European network, technological leads and first-mover advantages are strong in both networks. Networks have a tendency to become more centralized over time, with later entrants finding it harder to break into the core of the network. European firms which are entering the network at a later stage than their American counterparts may therefore simply be too late and it may be impossible for them to catch up with

American firms, especially those developing techniques close to the technological frontier, echoing another conclusion from Chapter 5. Moreover, the study found that over time these networks have tended to stabilize around a central core of firms, making it more and more difficult for firms to enter and grow within the industry. The study also concluded that the role performed by DBFs in the US could also conceivably be carried out through some other institutional arrangement which performed a bridging role between the large MNCs and the scientific base, although here the results were not conclusive as there are a number of firms which appear to be performing more than a simple bridging or technology transfer function.

However, in the long run, in an increasingly global economy, do national and regional networks really have much meaning? Do national strengths and weaknesses in science and technology matter a great deal or does research truly transcend national borders and overcome any weaknesses? Even if national research programmes remain important, as they undoubtedly will, can their weaknesses be overcome in part by importing and assimilating foreign technologies and skills, as has been done by a number of countries before, notably Japan? While a great deal of emphasis has been placed on the role of the DBF in the US and Europe, MNCs have dominated biotechnology R&D in Europe. Although the MNCs were in general slower to move into biotechnology research, their financial and scientific resources have placed them at the forefront of biotechnology R&D in Europe in recent years. The conclusions from Chapter 7 show that Europe's MNCs are increasingly tapping into the capabilities built up in the US network through strategic alliances with DBFs or by setting up laboratories in the US. The reasoning behind these investments was initially that the US was the largest market. An important effect instead has been to give access to these companies to the latest techniques which emerged and first diffused in the US.

Today these links with the US network are being used especially to build up capabilities which are at the forefront of biotechnology R&D such as gene therapy, genomics and combinatorial chemistry in which European companies are relatively weak. The study, however, also found that the opposite is occurring, namely the movement of corporate activities away from Europe to the US in a number of areas of European weakness, which is exacerbating the situation in Europe. Post-doctoral researchers are increasingly being attracted away from Europe to carry out research in the US, where the environment remains more attractive for biotechnology R&D, suggesting that Europe may still fall behind in the leading-edge technologies unless more is done to develop transparent and systematic Europe-wide regulations and to strengthen the research and training base, especially in terms of providing opportunities for young researchers.

The results obtained from this analysis of European research in leading-edge technologies were confirmed by the last study in the volume, on the commercialization gap in Europe in a key technology, namely gene therapy. In the case of basic research capabilities, it was found that although still at a disadvantage, European researchers were catching up with the US. This was evident from the numbers of papers published, especially in biomedical research, by European researchers. However, companies, especially dedicated gene therapy firms, were much slower to get started in Europe and remain smaller in number and firm size today. Even the investments made by European MNCs (which are substantial), tend to focus on the US network and US capabilities, pointing once again to a further weakening of the European research base. An interesting role has, however, emerged for European MNCs, which are increasingly tapping into the US research base, acquiring US-based DBFs, implying perhaps greater competitiveness for the European biotechnology industry through MNCs.

SOME PRELIMINARY CONCLUSIONS

The results discussed in this book have shown that European biotechnology lags behind the US in terms of absolute size and spending on R&D. Technical gaps have emerged in leading-edge and key techniques, largely, it appears, due to a lack of focus and contact with the commercial sector. The biotechnology industry in turn has been slower to develop new techniques and products, in part also because of this development gap between university and industry as well as the weaknesses of the financial and regulatory environments, which are considerably different in Europe than in the US. Nevertheless, while European companies may be starting from a lower base, this book has also highlighted changes in regulation, an easing of financial constraints, and increased collaboration between firms and universities, all of which have resulted in European biotechnology firms recording a larger number of successes in recent years. Europe may have started to close the research and industrial gap between itself and the US. A large number of remaining problems, were however, identified, and must be addressed by policy makers and industrialists alike in order to help companies narrow the gap with the US.

The State of Science

Most of the studies found that while in general Europe's scientific base remained strong, more could be done to identify and develop areas where leading-edge technologies were being developed and used. This requires a dynamic approach to funding scientific research and also comparable efforts to develop Europe's capabilities in developing linkages with the private sector in order to commercialize these scientific skills. Indeed the falling behind of Europe in the commercialization of biotechnology when compared with the US was confirmed by all the studies, especially as concerns some of the more advanced applications of biotechnology.

The State of the Innovation Environment

The creation of an environment supportive of commercialization is dependent on a number of factors. The regulatory and financial environment was cited by most of the studies as a major source of weakness in the commercialization of biotechnology in Europe. The issue of technology transfer and the commercialization or development gap between science and application were problems frequently cited by the firms interviewed. However, while it is evident that the lack of agreement in Europe about regulating GMO release and patenting has proved to be a disadvantage and must be addressed immediately, ways in which to close the equally disadvantageous commercialization gap are less obvious. There is a danger that in trying to close this gap, policy makers have conceptualized a linear relationship between scientific research conducted at universities, the DBF which often provides a bridging function, and the integrated company which develops and commercializes the product. To the contrary, the papers in this volume point out that the reasons for the success of industrial biotechnology in the US and a number of European countries have resulted from integrated research and complementary relationships between these actors.[3]

Thus instead of simply advocating the strengthening of basic research facilities or a more favourable financial environment for the DBF, this book has attempted to argue in favour of developing an integrated R&D system which recognizes the need to strengthen R&D capabilities among all the actors involved.

NOTES

1. The views expressed here are solely those of the author and should not be associated with the World Trade Organization, where she is currently a Trade Policy Analyst.
2. This may not always be the case. For example, Japanese firms built up significant capabilities in technologies they were relatively weak in, by forming strategic alliances with research groups in other countries, notably the USA.
3. The conclusions also serve to confirm what has been pointed out earlier by a number of studies on technological change (see, for example, Freeman, 1982 among others).

REFERENCES

Department of Trade and Industry (1995), *Annual Report*, London: DTI.

Freeman, C. (1982), *The Economics of Industrial Innovation*, London: Pinter Publishers.

Ward, M. (1995), 'Should the FDA emulate Europe's EMEA?', *Bio/Technology*, **13**(7), 636–8.

Ward, M. (1996), 'Another push to revise Eurobiotech Directives', *Bio/Technology*, **14**(2), 133–4.

Bibliography

Abric, J.C. (1987), *Coopération, Compétition et Représentations Sociales*, Fribourg: Ed. Del Val.

Acha, V. (1997), 'Policy development under uncertainty', in Part 4, TU870, *Capacities for Managing Development*, London: Sage Publications.

Acharya, R., A. Arundel and L. Orsenigo (1996), *The Evolving Structure of the European Biotechnology Industry and its Future Competitiveness*. Final Report for the Biotechnology Programme (BIOTECH) of the European Community, DG XII, the Netherlands: MERIT, University of Limburg.

Advisory Council for the Applied Research and Development/Advisory Board for the Research Councils/The Royal Society (1980), *Biotechnology. Report of a Joint Working Party*, London: HMSO.

Advisory Council on Science and Technology (1994), *Technology Foresight. The Identification and Promotion of Emerging and Generic Technologies*, London: HMSO.

Ahern, R. (1993), 'Implications of strategic alliances for small R&D-intensive firms', *Environment and Planning A*, **25**(10), 1511–26.

Amin, M. (1996), 'Understanding "strategic alliances": the limit of transaction cost economics', in R. Coombs, A. Richards, P. Saviotti and V. Walsh (eds), *Technological Collaboration: The Dynamics of Cooperation in Industrial Innovation*, Aldershot: Edward Elgar, pp. 165–79.

Anon. (1996), 'Another chance for bio-patenting', *Research Fortnight*, 16 October, 14–15.

Arora, A. and A. Gambardella (1990), 'Complementarity and external linkages: the strategies of the large firms in biotechnology', *Journal of Industrial Economics*, **38**(4), 361–79.

Arthur, W.B. (1989), *Silicon Valley Locational Clusters: When Do Increasing Returns Imply Monopoly?*, Working Paper 89-007, Santa Fe Institute.

Assouline, G. and J. Chataway (1995), *Global Industrial Competition and European Biotechnology Research and Innovation: Policy, Limits, Constraints and Priorities*. Energy and Research Series Working Paper W-17, Luxembourg: European Parliament.

Audretsch, D.B. (1995), *Innovation and Industry Evolution*, Cambridge, MA: MIT Press.

Audretsch, D.B. and M.P. Feldman (1994), *R&D Spillovers and the Geography of Innovation and Production*, Berlin: Wissenschaftzentrum Berlin für Sozialforschung (WZB), Working Paper.

Audretsch, D.B. and P. Stephan (1994), *Company Scientists' Locational Links: The Case of Biotechnology*, Mimeo, Berlin: Wissenschaftzentrum Berlin für Sozialforschung and Palo Alto: Center for Economic Policy Research, Stanford University, CA.

Bank of England (1996), *The Financing of Technology-Based Small Firms*, London: Bank of England.

BMFT (Der Bundesminister für Forschung und Technologie) (1989), *Programmreport Biotechnologie*, Bonn: BMFT.

BMFT (Der Bundesminister für Forschung und Technologie) (1993), *Bundesbericht Forschung*, Bonn: BMFT.

Bullock, W.O. and M.D. Dibner (1995), 'The state of the US biotechnology industry', *TIBTECH*, **13**, 463–7.

Burt, R.S. (1980), 'Models of network structure', *Annual Review of Sociology*, **6**, 79-141.

Cabinet Office (1993), *Realising Our Potential: A Strategy for Science, Engineering and Technology*, CM2250, London: HMSO.

Callon, M. (1991), 'Réseaux technico-économiques et irréversibilités', in R. Boyer (ed.), *Les Figures de l'Irréversibilité en Economie*, Paris: Editions de l'Ecole des Hautes Etudes en Sciences Sociales, pp. 195–230.

Chataway, J. (1992), *The Making of Biotechnology: A Case Study of Radical Innovation*, PhD Thesis, Milton Keynes: Open University.

Chataway, J. and J. Tait (1993), 'Risk regulation and strategic decision making in biotechnology: the political economy of innovation', *Agriculture and Human Values*, **10**(2), 60–67.

Chataway, J., G. Assouline and G. Ruivenkamp (1996), *Risk Perception, Regulation and the Management of Agro-Biotechnologies*, Final Report for the Biotechnology Programme (BIOTECH) of the European Community, DG XII, Swavesey: Segal Quince Wickstead.

Chesnais, F. (1988), 'Technical cooperation agreement between independent firms, novel issues for economic analysis and the formulation of national technological policies', *STI Review*, No. 4, 51–120.

Chesnais, F. and V. Walsh (1994), *Biotechnology and the Chemical Industry: The Relevance of Some Evolutionary Concepts*, paper presented at the EUNETIC Conference, Strasbourg, 6–8 October.

Christou, P., N. Carey, H. Brunner et al. (1996), *Evaluation of the BRIDGE Programme (1990–1994)*, EUR 16650 EN, Luxembourg: Office for Official Publications of the European Communities.

CNER (Comité National d'Evaluation de la Recherche) (1994), *Un Autre Regard sur la Recherche, Sept Evaluations 1990–1993*, partie 7 Evaluation du programme 'Biotechnologie', Paris: La Documentation Française.

Cohen, M. and D. Levinthal (1989), 'Innovation and learning: the two faces of R&D', *Economic Journal*, **99**(397), 569–96.

Cohen, M. and D. Levinthal (1990), 'Absorptive capacity: a new perspective on learning and innovation', *Administrative Science Quarterly*, **35**(1), 128–52.

Commission of the European Communities (1993), *Growth, Competitiveness, Employment: The Challenges and Ways Forward into the 21st Century*, White Paper COM (93) 700 final, Brussels: CEC.

Commission of the European Communities (1994) *Biotechnology and the White Paper on Growth Competitiveness and Employment: Preparing the Next Stage*, com (94) 219 final, Brussels: CEC.

Coombs, J. and Y.R. Alston (eds) (1995), *International Biotechnology Directory*, London: Macmillan Reference.

Craig, R. (1994), *Exploitation of LCR Technology*, Presentation to MRC Conference on the Successful Exploitation of Biomedical Research, 7–8 March, Regents College, London.

Crespi, R.S. (1993), 'Protecting biotechnological inventions', *Chemistry & Industry*, No. 10, 363–6.

De Looze, M.A., J. Estades, P. B. Joly, S. Ramani, P.P. Saviotti, J. Senker and J.L. Pedersen (1996), *The Role of SMEs/DBFs in Technology Creation and Diffusion: Implications for European Competitiveness in Biotechnology*. A report for the European Commission, CT-942032, Grenoble: INRA-SERD.

Department of Trade and Industry (1995), *Annual Report*, London: DTI.

Dibner, M.D. (1995a), *Biotechnology Guide USA*, 3rd Edition, Research Triangle Park, NC: Institute for Biotechnology Information.

Dibner, M.D. (1995b), 'Biotech centers represent a major force in development and support of industry', *Genetic Engineering News*, **15**(17), 4.

Edgington, S. (1995), 'Germany: a dominant force by the year 2000?', *Bio/Technology*, **13**(8), 752–6.

EMEA (European Medicines Evaluation Agency) (1996), *Directory*, Luxembourg: Office for Official Publications of the European Communities.

Ernst & Young (1994), *European Biotech 94. A New Industry Emerges*, London: Ernst & Young International.

Ernst & Young (1995), *European Biotech 95. Gathering Momentum*, London: Ernst & Young International.

Ernst & Young (1996), *European Biotech 96. Volatility and Value*, London: Ernst & Young International.

Escourrou, N. (1992), 'Les societés de biotechnologie européennes: un réseau très imbriqué', *Biofutur*, July–August, 40–42.

EZ (Ministerie van Economische Zaken) (1994), *Biotechnologiebeleid: Van Onderzoek naar Markt*, Den Haag: Project Groep Biotechnologie, MEZ.

Florida, R.L. and M. Kenney (1988), 'Venture capital-financed innovation and technological change in the USA', *Research Policy*, **17**(3), 119–37.

Forrest, J.E. and J.C. Martin (1992), 'Strategic alliances between large and small research intensive organizations: experiences in the biotechnology industry', *R&D Management*, **22**(1), 41–53.

Freeman, C. (1982), *The Economics of Industrial Innovation*, London: Pinter Publishers.

Gambardella, A. (1995), *Science and Innovation in the US Pharmaceutical Industry*, Cambridge: Cambridge University Press.

Gebbart, F. (1993), 'The Netherlands pursues the goal of becoming Europe's biotechnology delta', *Genetic Engineering News*, 15 May, 12–13.

Gort, M. and S. Klepper (1982), 'Time paths in the diffusion of product innovations', *Economic Journal*, **92**(367), 630–53.

Grabowsky, H. and J. Vernon (1994), 'Innovation and structural change in pharmaceuticals and biotechnology', *Industrial and Corporate Change*, **3**(2), 435–49.

Greenpeace (1996), Press release on GMOs, 6 November, Paris.

Griffin, J.P. (1995), 'The EMEA – Euromouse or white elephant?', *Scrip Magazine*, March, 9–10.

Hagedoorn, J. and S. Huibers (1995), *The Evolving Structure of the Biotechnology Industry and its Future Competitiveness: Strategic Alliances*, Maastricht: MERIT, University of Limburg.

Hagedoorn, J. and J. Schakenraad (1990), 'Inter-firm partnerships and cooperative strategies in core technologies', in C. Freeman and L. Soete (eds), *New Explorations in the Economics of Technological Change*, London: Pinter Publishers.

Hagedoorn, J. and J. Schakenraad (1992), 'Intercompany cooperation and technological developments – leading companies and networks of strategic alliances in information technologies', *Research Policy*, **21**(2), 163–90.

Håkansson, P., H. Kjellberg and A. Lundgren (1993), 'Strategic alliances in global biotechnology – a network approach', *International Business Review*, **2**, 65–82.

Henderson, R.M. (1993), 'Underinvestment and incompetence as responses to radical innovation – evidence from the photolithographic alignment equipment industry', *Rand Journal of Economics*, **24**(2), 248–70.

Henderson, R. (1994), 'The evolution of integrative competence: innovation in cardiovascular drug discovery', *Industrial and Corporate Change*, **3**(3), 607–30.

Hodgson, J. (1994), 'The end of French biotechnology R&D?', *Bio/Technology Europroduct Focus*, Spring, 5.

Holzman, D. (1995), 'Political consensus to bring reform by spring', *Chemistry & Industry*, No. 20, 823.

House of Lords Select Committee on Science and Technology (1993), *Regulation of the United Kingdom Biotechnology Industry and Global Competitiveness*, HL Papers 80-I and 80-II, London: HMSO.

Informal Consultation Group on Biotechnology (1995), *Market Introduction and Labelling of Foods Produced with the Aid of Modern Biotechnology (Genetic Modification)*, The Netherlands.

Irvine, J., B. Martin and P. Isard (1990), *Investing in the Future. An International Comparison of Government Funding of Academic and Related Research*, Aldershot: Edward Elgar.

Jaeckel, G., B. Husing, E. Strauss and T. Reiss (1994), *Analyse der Baden-Württembergischen F&E-Strukturen und -Potentiale in der Biotechnologie*. Studie im Auftrag der Akademie für Technikfolgenabschätzung in Baden-Württemberg, Karlsruhe, Germany: ISI.

Jaffe, A.B. (1986), 'Technological opportunities and spillovers of R&D: evidence from the firms' patents, profits and market value', *American Economic Review*, **76**, 984–1001.

Jaffe, A.B., M. Trajtenberg and R. Henderson (1993), 'Geographic localization of knowledge spillovers as evidenced by patent citations', *Quarterly Journal of Economics*, **100**(3), 577–98.

Joly, P.B. and C. Ducos (1993), *Les Artifices du Vivant: Stratégies d'Innovation dans l'Industrie des Semences*, Paris: INRA-Economica.

Jones, N.R.N. (1994), 'Relaxing European regulations', *Bio/Technology*, **12**(11), 1144.

Kenney, M. (1986), *Biotechnology: The University–Industry Complex*, New Haven. Conn.: Yale University Press.

Kidd, G. and J. Dvorak (1994), 'A gutsy map of the future of agbiotech', *Bio/Technology*, **12**(11), 1064–5.

Klepper, S. (1992), *Entry, Exit and Innovation over the Product Life Cycle: The Dynamics of First Mover Advantages, Declining Product Innovation and Market Failure*, paper presented at the International J.A. Schumpeter Society, Kyoto, August.

Kraus, M. (1994), *Regulation and Competitiveness of the European Biotechnology Industry*, Working Paper, Luxembourg: Directorate General for Research, European Parliament.

Krugman, P. (1991), *Geography and Trade*, Cambridge, MA: MIT Press.

Levidow, L., S. Carr, R. von Schomberg and D. Wield (1996), 'Regulating agricultural biotechnology in Europe: harmonisation difficulties, opportunities, dilemmas', *Science and Public Policy*, **23**(3), 135–57.

Liebeskind, J.P., A.L. Oliver, L.G. Zucker and M.B. Brewer (1995), *Social Networks, Learning and Flexibility: Sourcing Scientific Knowledge in New Biotechnology Firms*, NBER Working Paper 5320, Cambridge, MA: National Bureau of Economic Research.

Malerba, F. and L. Orsenigo (1995), 'Schumpeterian patterns of innovation', *Cambridge Journal of Economics*, **19**(1), 47–65.

Malerba, F. and L. Orsenigo (1996), 'Schumpeterian patterns of innovation are technology-specific', *Research Policy*, **25**(3), 451–78.

Malmborg, C., P. Feillet, F. Kafatos, J. Koeman, P. Saviotti, G. Schmidt-Kastner and G. Walker (1988), *Evaluation of the Biomolecular Programme – BEP (1982–1986) and the Biotechnology Action Programme – BAP (1985–1989)*, Luxembourg: Commission of the European Communities.

Manigart, S. (1994), 'The founding rate of venture capital firms in three European countries (1970–1990)', *Journal of Business Venturing*, **9**(6), 525–41.

Marshall, A. (1920), *Principles of Economics*, 8th Edition, London: Macmillan.

Martin, P.A. (1995), 'The American gene therapy industry and the social shaping of a new technology', *The Genetic Engineer and Biotechnologist*, **15**, 155.

Martin, P.A. and S.M. Thomas (1996), *The Development of Gene Therapy in Europe and the United States: A Comparative Analysis*, Final Report for the Biotechnology Programme (BIOTECH) of the European Community, DG XII, STEEP Special Report No. 5, Brighton: Science Policy Research Unit, University of Sussex.

McCain, K.W. (1995), 'The structure of biotechnology R&D', *Scientometrics*, **32**(2), 153–75.

McKelvey, M. (1994), *Evolutionary Innovation: Early Industrial Uses of Genetic Engineering*, S-581 83, Linköping, Sweden: Department of Technology and Social Change, Linköping University.

Mustar, P. (1995), *Science et Innovation. Annuaire Raisonné de la Création d'Entreprises par les Chercheurs*, Paris: Economica.

Mytelka, L.K. (ed.) (1991), *Strategic Partnership and the World Economy*, London: Pinter Publishers.

National Science Board (1993), *Science and Engineering Indicators – 1993*, Washington, DC: US Government Printing Office.

Oakey, R., W. Faulkner, S. Cooper and V. Walsh (1990), *New Firms in the Biotechnology Industry*, London: Pinter Publishers.

Orsenigo, L. (1989), *The Emergence of Biotechnology: Institutions and Markets in Industrial Innovation*, London: Pinter Publishers.

Penrose, E. (1959), *The Theory of the Growth of the Firm*, Oxford: Blackwell.

Pisano, G. (1991), 'The governance of innovation: vertical integration and collaborative arrangements in the biotechnology industry', *Research Policy*, **20**(3), 237–49.

Powell, W. (1990), 'Neither market nor hierarchy: network forms of organization', in B.N. Straw and L.L. Cummings (eds), *Research in Organizational Behavior*, 12, pp. 295–336.

Prahalad, C.K. and G. Hamel (1990), 'The core competence of the corporation', *Harvard Business Review*, May–June, 79–91.

Ramani, S. (1995), 'The French evolution of biotechnology', *Bio/Technology*, **13**(8), 757–9.

Rip, A. and L. Courtial (1984), 'Co-word maps of biotechnology: an example of cognitive scientometrics', *Scientometrics*, **6**(6), 381–400.

Rothwell, R. and W. Zegveld (1982), *Innovation and the Small and Medium Sized Firm*, London: Pinter Publishers.

SAGB (1990), *Community Policy for Biotechnology: Economic Benefits and European Competitiveness*, Brussels: CEFIC.

SAGB (1994), *Biotechnology Policy in the European Union: Prescriptions for Growth, Competitiveness and Employment*, Brussels: CEFIC.

Saviotti, P.P. (1996), *Technological Evolution, Variety and the Economy*, Aldershot: Edward Elgar.

Schilperoort, R.A. (1982), *Innovatie Programme Biotechnologie*, Voorlichtingsdienst, The Hague: Wietenschapsbelerd.

Schumpeter, J.A. (1912), *The Theory of Economic Development*, reprinted (1934), Cambridge, MA: Harvard University Press.

Scott-Ram, N. and A.G. Sheard (1995), 'The rise and fall of the EU patent directive', *Bio/Technology*, **13**(8), 734–5.

Senker, J. (1996), 'National systems of innovation, organizational learning and industrial biotechnology', *Technovation*, **16**(5), 219–29.

Senker, J. and M. Sharp (1988), *The Biotechnology Directorate of the SERC. Report and Evaluation of its Achievements – 1981–87*, Report to the Management Committee of the Biotechnology Directorate, Brighton: Science Policy Research Unit, University of Sussex.

Senker, J. and M. Sharp (1997), 'Organisational learning in cooperative alliances: some case studies in biotechnology', *Technology Analysis & Strategic Management*, **9**(1), 35–51.

Senker, J., P.-B. Joly and M. Reinhard (1996), *Overseas Biotechnology Research by Europe's Chemical/Pharmaceuticals Multinationals: Rationale and Implications*, Final Report for the Biotechnology Programme (BIOTECH) of the European Community, DG XII, STEEP Discussion Paper No. 33, Brighton: Science Policy Research Unit, University of Sussex.

Shackley, S. (1993), *Regulating the New Biotechnologies in Europe*, DPhil Thesis, Brighton: University of Sussex.

Shackley, S. and J. Hodgson (1991), 'Biotechnology Regulation in Europe', *Bio/Technology*, **9**(11), 1056–61.

Sharp, M. (1985a), *The New Biotechnology: European Governments in Search of a Strategy*, Brighton: Sussex European Papers, University of Sussex.

Sharp, M. (1985b), 'Biotechnology: watching and waiting', in M. Sharp (ed.), *Europe and the New Technologies*, London: Pinter Publishers, pp. 161–212.

Sharp, M. (forthcoming), 'The Science of Nations: European Multinationals and American Biotechnology', *International Journal of Technology Management* (Biotechnology Review).

Sharp, M., S. Thomas and P. Martin (1993), *Technology Transfer and Innovation Policy: Chemicals and Biotechnology*, STEEP Discussion Paper No. 6, Brighton: Science Policy Research Unit, University of Sussex.

Shohet, S. (1996), 'Biotechnology in Europe: contentions in the risk regulation debate', *Science and Public Policy*, **23**(2), 117–22.

Sveinsdottir, S. (1995), 'Bridge to biodevelopment', *Bio/Technology*, **13**(8), 763–4.

Tait, J. (1990), *Biotechnology. Interactions between Technology, Environment and Society*, Technology Policy Group, Occasional Paper 20, Milton Keynes: Open University.

Tait, J. and L. Levidow (1992), 'Proactive and reactive approaches to regulation: the case of biotechnology', *Futures*, **24**(3), 219–31.

Teece, D. (1986), 'Profiting from technological innovation', *Research Policy*, **15**(6), 285–305.

Tils, C. (1995), *Dutch Biotechnology Policy. A Practical Network Approach for Companies, Government and Societal Groups*, Den Haag: Rathenau Institute.

Tushman, M.L. and P. Anderson (1986), 'Technological discontinuities and organizational environments', *Administrative Science Quarterly*, **31**(3), 439–65.

Unterhuber, R.J. and I.E. Furst (1996), 'Gene therapy goes commercial in Germany with entrance of startup firms', *Genetic Engineering News*, **15**(3), 1.

US Congress, Office of Technology Assessment (1991), *Biotechnology in a Global Economy*, Washington, DC: US Government Printing Office.

Walsh, V., J. Niosi and P. Mustar (1995), 'Small-firm formation in biotechnology: a comparison of France, Britain and Canada', *Technovation*, **15**, 303–27.

Ward, M. (1995a), 'Should the FDA emulate Europe's EMEA?', *Bio/Technology*, **13**(7), 636–8.

Ward, M. (1995b), 'In Germany, biotech resistance leads to progress', *Bio/Technology*, **13**(10), 1048–9.

Ward, M. (1996), 'Another push to revise Eurobiotech directives', *Bio/Technology*, **14**(2), 133–4.

Winter, S.G. (1984), 'Schumpeterian competition in alternative technological regimes', *Journal of Economic Behaviour and Organizations*, **5**(3–4), 287–320.

Zechendorf, B. (1994), 'What the public thinks about biotechnology', *Bio/Technology*, **12**(9), 870–75.

Index